v v v

A Poetry Garden

v v v

Preface

Creating poetry is like gardening – seeds of inspiration from a journal, time and thought and editing to help them grow. Later comes the revisiting of older plants and the removal of weeds and thinning of plants when they become too thick.

I invite you to walk through this garden with me – see the bright flowers, the thick dark soil as it nourishes life. Words have power, and we share that power with the hope our words will inspire you to write or enjoy life more vividly.

Contents

[Russell W. Beckett]

Knuckled White

hammer down and knuckles white
on the torture wheel again
leaving behind a rooster tail
of cremation ashes and bone dust
roaring into the night on penitent dreams
hoping to conceal visions of vapor lock
praying for the pavement
of a miracle mile

I scry out corn leaves
at the bottom of my empty whiskey glass
this mosaic of future memory clinging
lit up in a break of neon gas
to be laid like a royal flush of
honky-tonk kings scepter and orb
while hiding behind the flutter of bat wings
jilted jukebox queens

color a rainbow from the reflection
where convict bottles hang heads
to be buried dead man deep
six feet, seven, alms at the crossroad
goading a midnight devil
come to the confessional like a priest

ready for the breaking of vows of silence
for a pale mutiny passing

hammer down and knuckles white
gripping the torture wheel again
leaving behind a wake of bottles of absinthe
in rear viewed mirrors
screeching into the night
penitent dreams hoping to reveal
an answer written, hidden
between lines of graffiti on bathroom walls

another rest stop on the highway
lit only by a singular sodium lamp
scribbled missives litter the ground
on discarded chewing gum wrappers
like missing pieces to a cryptographic puzzle
from a veiled traveler's ghost
ciphers to epitaphs given
to the hands of a cruel wind blowing

paint the canvas with baptismal oils
the gaudy sacrament of hues
in portraits of nothing men hidden
and nothing women in fancy dress
for walls of emptied diners
the kingdom of the greasy spoons
nursing away the cost of the gun barrel round
bullet of the last call

hammer down and knuckles white
spinning the torture wheel again
horizon egressing from the fasting of a sun
come to eat night away
catching glimpses of strangers to the slipstream,
drifting in a mirage, obscured and camouflaged
by streaks on windowed eyes of empty passengers

baring teeth and mouth opening
to taste the asphalt of this road
taking in a filling of whispering tires
from the feast of lust banquets
static electricity arcing out from the radio
stationary and untuned
the song of check out time
passing from solicitous motel rooms

color a globe filigree
vacant rust longitude and latitude lines
spinning yarns while the crochet unravels
into tribes of bending backs
heaving away the sack of peddlers
damned by the traps of a season
to an auction gavel being beaten,
lost and grasping fingers of night's despair.

R.W. Beckett is a from San Antonio (but forever a California
boy). He writes poetry to make people think. He is an avid video
game enthusiast and art film lover. Allpoetry.com/R.W.Beckett

[Carl Wayne Jent]

Broken Mind Mending

Many demon days I lost on parchment pathway
would climb the slate-stained stone stairs my way
framed by grandma and grandpa's perfume portrait
to arrive at charcoal shelter created by my mind's mental state

To stay tucked in the backyards of my bisque mind
where the sweet chrome kaleidoscope I would find
a place where the red robin's honeydew egg hatches
and my artichoke mental clusters receive clementine patches

A month of catching comfort in the crevice of the cerebellum
has brought bloom to branch that bordered the brains problem
allowing my eggshell whites of radish eyes to gaze at gazebo garden
and fly into air to stare bouquets blossoms with butterflies' pardon

To see cornucopia of flamingo colors that dot edge of brook's bank
while burgundy bluebonnets flowers give us turquoise water to thank
as the wind caress the giant cypress wood with its mantis feel
listening to the blackbirds and mulberry woodpecker's squeal

Sit at cherry bar at my cadmium condo beside cobblestone fireplace
admiring asparagus clover colored valley with its heavenly taste
below god's goldenrod rays showing pumpkin and mango grace
remembering two teenagers laughing as we marched in place

Pregnant mate and I, lie against post, snipping the snapdragon
watching squirrels being attacked from both sides as war rages on

the chocolate owls commands robins seeing hyacinth on tree trunk
as the inchworm ivy hangs to blackberry hedges hiding skunk

While the still teal streams reflect like jewel glass before supper
hearing taps of shrubs dropping the roses peddles like rubber
having scaled the walls of dire depressive depths to regain life
yearn to return to love that burns from lost child and adoring wife

---

The poems I write, I write for comfort. I read and ponder life's journey and feel a little better about my existence. Life is grand and I cherish each breath. Allpoetry.com/Waynejent

[Kristof Domšić]

Erotic imprint

Her hazel eyes in a narrative expression
ripples her pelvis with of an eventful in cobra
and my daring tongue high in feast, will slash her
on her crown in active madness object

swirling around her carousel, I siphon
its castle blooming in a pink september fruit
softening her contours without shame, she dares
offer myself this little lick, of fall bark

I am the spirit of the woods, morning, july, gladiolus
parameter profound in violet in her clammy-eye
existence ultimate, exit, from my refinement

new horizon of a glossy taste on music
it will be price for her young age
in the sense of a complete geodesic work

Érotique empreinte

Ses yeux noisette en une expression narrative
Ondoie son bassin d'un mouvementé en cobra
Et ma langue audace haute en festin la sabra
Sur sa couronne en objet marais folie active

Tournoyant dans tout son carrousel, je siphonne
Son château fleuri en un fruit septembre rose

Adoucissant ses contours sans pudeur, elle ose
M'offrir ce petit lécher d'écorce d'automne

Je suis esprit des bois, matin juillet glaïeul
Profond paramètre en violette en son moite oeil
Ultime existence exit de mon tout affinage

Nouvel horizon d'un goût lustré en musique
Elle n'aura de prix que pour son jeune âge
Aux sens d'une oeuvre complète géodésique

My name is Chris, I'm living in Paris, France. Here on alloetry,
I'm writing things like since je is 2, a story of love, natures,
personnal and sometimes, something dark in 150 grains of
melancholy. Allpoetry.com/Chris-Charmer

[Robert Poleski]

Spring meadow

again
spring begins
nature's defibrillator
jump starts life into the land
blossom by blossom
spring flowers ripple
paint laughing soil
makes your heart sing
still chilly at night
spring begins
purified meadow's air
brings new life and new hope is born

the dawn moon's bright sheen
covers malachite green grass
yipping fox cubs break
the quiet of the world
as the moon begins to wane
fog of flowers on the field
starts reveal itself
their aroma hovering
around the meadow
spears of morning light
drench the farthest corners
with their golden magic
purple crocuses

glow with royal pride
pleased with their grandeur
jewel green grasshoppers
bounce atop the grass
like leggy trampolines

murmuration of starlings
wheel and bank overhead
like wind-tossed gunpowder
high octane rhythm
throbs and thumps
symphony of sound
spirit renewing rustic scene
on a spring meadow

Spring in the garden

spring is here
in your garden
cauterizing gaping wounds
winter left behind
world moving
from iron grey to fairyland green
peppermint grass
the best nature surgeon

harp strings of golden light
squeeze through
naked cherry tree branches
shamelessly exposing

its budding buds
manicured with bliss pink petals
then touch steaming shadows and soften the frozen earth
for future occupants
of this shadowy corner
shoals of honeysuckle
primroses and bluebells
sway and weave a rich mosaic
crocuses and daffodils
add to the stained-glass perfection
all waving at the ecstasy blue sky
in sunny garden's corner

overhead
honking geese whooping swans
from winter exodus
of banished birds
flowing out of Celtic fairytale
thumb-plump bumblebees
loot from honeypots of mustard-yellow flowers
mini tumble dryers
plunging their syringes
extracting their booty

spring is here
in the distance
world's greatest sound
coming out of hibernation
mellifluous hum of a lawnmower surrogate wind music
flowing into winter-battered ears

whittling and shearing the grass
pedicuring a symmetrical perfection
erasing winter's untidy
jumble sale of chaos
leaving their clippings behind
for the fussy nesters
the air smells like
roasted sugar cakes
after the grass is shorn
baked oven smell of grass
as the sun purges it of water
young and lush

spring is here
bountiful garden again
spirit enriching
pastoral scenes
nature's grand theatre
the pumping heart of nature
is beating again
right here
in the garden
saying
let's party again

————————————

What I see is my own world, my whole intimate universe, with
my mind, my heart, looking inside things, inside feelings, what
makes it laugh or cry, love or hate, what makes it feel pleasure or
pain. Allpoetry.com/Robert_Poleski

[Marilyn Griffin]

harnessed

I'm guilty of harnessing joy
clipping on a leash,
and taking it for a walk
through tidy streets
past the thin trees
with white bark,
the etched eyes
that stare at me in patches,
their trunks protruding from
foot high wrought-iron fences

In the city of Orange
corner turns okay
only
on the green light
near the traffic circle

no trash in the gutters
by O'Hara's pub
and on the curb by
the beer truck entrance
my husband-then-boyfriend's name
carved in the once new cement

Guido was the King of Easy Street

after the rain,
the sidewalks shiny
but not slippery or wet-
no puddles
or dark skies hovering
holding heavy gray lint clouds

no latinos staring from
streaked and grimy upper windows
or retired professors of literature or psychology
sneaking out of sorority houses and

flapping their narcissism
in lecture halls
in their musty jackets with leather elbow patches
a crisp wind of themselves
circling in tiny hurricanes

it's a short walk-

sometimes,
I let go off leash-
hoping beyond hope
that it isn't smashed to smithereens
by the frat boys

or that it falls
between the cracks in the sidewalk-
a thin glee screaming as it's

washed down the gutters under the 22
to the 405

by the rain
to the sea

_____

An avid reader, a gardener and a wrangler of ducks and words,
Marilyn lives on her farm with all the happy little critters. Thanks
to AP, she occasionally writes as well.
Allpoetry.com/Greeningofautumn

[Joan Rooney]

Eilat Upon the Red Sea

Bobbing sailboats surround a golden beach
and dazzling ziggurats,
hotels of cubic forms, and tropical plants
aline a palm-lined boulevard.

The jagged crags of the pink Moav Hills encircle
a marina and glittering lagoon lit
with glistening jewels, like gems gifted perhaps
from Solomon to the Queen of Sheba.

From here the azure waters fringed with coral reefs
flow southward toward the Gulf of Aqaba,
to the Straits of Tiran and into the Red Sea
where Sheba set sail for the land of Ophir.

I'm a retired librarian living in Ottawa Canada. I have done a lot of genealogical research for myself and others. I am interested in photography and I have written poems for over 25 years now. Allpoetry.com/Joan_Rooney

[Brooke K. Higgins]

Equinox

Light blares through
a crack between Venetian shields,
An adamant searchlight
floods the piles.
Sloughed off dirty clothes, soiled tissues, and
filthy dishes teetering in sloppy towers
smother the nightstand,
dresser top,
encircle the bed,
entombing my animated corpse.

It burns.
Mandibular gnawing from a sea of red ants
lifts me to move,
goads me to my feet,
exposing the reek of seventeen days
at the knees of a silent deity.

Limbs stiffened from disuse stumble,
quaking at thoughts of exposure.
Impersonal stripping of soap
surfacting a shell of grime,
oil layers and dirt
slipping down my thighs.

Clean, naked -
starkly vulnerable.
Craving a return to the cave,
the hovel of self-loathing.
Grimacing a smile,
breaking the crust,
stretching to make pliable
clay from a mound of dirt.

A personal spring
forced by an equinox,
serendipitously timed with the rain.
Scent of Ishtar
vining into my nostrils,
calling for a smile to bloom.

Brooke is a 30-something year-old woman trapped in a healthy
marriage who copes with anxiety, depression, and the occasional
zest for life. Allpoetry.com/Babbler

[Roger E. Miller]

a farm awakens in the dark

the wind moans through the sides of the barn
as though some boards had become reeds
and the barn itself the wood section of an orchestra

the low moo of cows
become the base of the French horn section

the horse neighing
like the high pitch of a piccolo

a maiden collecting eggs
her soprano becomes opera
paced by the metronomic clucks of the hens

a bull bellows in baritone
as the rooster crows to the sun
'wake up, I command you'

the tractor now quiet
will soon be coughing like an old man
smoking in puffs
as it chugs along

over in the farm house
the kitchen widows turn yellow with light
through them
the farmer's wife can be seen
readying the table for the first meal of the day

I am 'freewit' from Michigan. I am happy to be one of millions of poets. We can help show what 'tis and what's taint. The reader's mind is our canvas where we use words like an artist uses paint.
Allpoetry.com/freewit

[Alwyn Barddylbach]

The Kymin (Cae-y-Maen)

Up and down Gwên's rustic vales
in sorrow wood and mossy den
where badgers, sheep and cattle brood
all imbued in oak and sycamore,
upon this sunny hill descend.

For that is my presumption
the poem plain, let's appreciate the moment
just being, not prise any deaf advantage
nor defend an idle sun's contemplative shadow
mere god's themselves pretend?

Suspend the pastel life of solitude,
the long and lonely sunscape in our windowpane and
touch, behold so much retain that part of you and me;
in mountain's giant boots, in raincloud's weather graze
so shall I grow old on gratitude.

Then let me take you to Trafalgar
through poppy fields of Agincourt,
far above the Wye upon that hill
where Troddi and the Mynwy meet,
castles mournful mill.

In humble tethered woodland here we stand,
ghosts of Mabinogian, princely folly, sword and rook,

babbling lark and naval english temple thrill;
beyond this wild and rugged kingdom, west of Usk
hollow stony Marches, the dorms of Wales.

Above me stars toil by night. I'll show you
a universe of cosmic cloud and pure delight,
true kinship, being not believing vaguely out of sight,
frontier worlds unseen spoiling in fountains of light;
and I saw a thousand ships so bright.

But in my luminary cavern dwell,
in valleys west and evergreen
and far above the Wye upon that hill,
the best beneath the Kymin flow,
the Monnow of the Dean.

For that is my presumption gladly still,
bewitched these days of idle sun, of ashen haze,
mountain brook and heather in king Arthur's southern gaze,
sunscaped meadows; then dream but once again of this
my love, our beloved home and country.

———————————

View from a hill - historic town, foothills and garden valleys of the
Forest of Dean and Welsh mountains. A confluence of 3 rivers,
stone castles, pastoral farms and landscapes, Monmouth, Wales
Allpoetry.com/Barddylbach

[Herb Mitchell]

Fowlers Bed (Tainted Natures Fleece)

By the river stands of sycamore, shelter from rain,
grim stately in visible camouflage bark suits,
limbs cloaked in greenish browned curling leaves,
an over winterer's harvest, birds love rolled button baller's fruit.

Ironclad in graffiti by swank an old passenger train's fate,
hollowed neighbor to mallards, gulls and geese,
cement slabs lay adorning in a shallow river's stead,
worn architecture of man is a fowlers bed, tainted natures fleece.

Natures laws awareness is oblivious to bridges,
fire hose draped engines, wood benches and lamps,
bored holes planted stars and stripes rugged vital,
city sidewalks poured anew brick paths weaved neatly in plaid,
a man made nature trail of gravel, dirt grass and pressed vinyl.

A dahlia bloom staked claim to first under a cherry tree,
burning bush as autumn fell in red neon glow,
a pollinating bee lands to feed on flowers nectar,
a natural fuel more potent than sweet sorghum.

Trekking through town up down around city streets,
for a moment by the river stopped took a seat,
nature's beauty will forever not be tidy and neat,
construction cannot with Gods' creation, compete.

My name is Herb learned I could write in 2010. I enjoy trying to find different ways to describe things. Especially beauty, the sun. You're never quite sure if you'll get served unleaded moonshine. Allpoetry.com/HerbM

[Robert Poleski]

Ocean's Showcase

A sunny seaside afternoon

living by the sea shore
I enjoy walking miles
on a sunny summer afternoons
overlooking the west facing long beach
curving along the ocean's edge

above
the incessant blanket of neon blue sky
laced with cherub white clouds
along the limitless horizon's arch
swallows arrowing through the air
in pirouetting ballet chasing insects
wolf-white seagulls lounging on the nearby craggy cliffs
patrolling the beach for easy snacks
others circling and gliding in the air
hunting for fish
stealing from fishing boats beneath them
bobbing and dipping in the waves
zephyr breeze carries a refreshing mist of salty droplets
reflected from rocks nearby
right into my face

a rhythmic metronomic pulse of a sleepy sea
leavening like a slow rising dough

kindles its own symphony
murmuring of the seductive blue waves
rolling with its own majesty
with hypnotic mesmerizing
sighing and splashing
trembling and throbbing
whirring as soft as a lullaby
crawling steadily to the shore
gently dousing the beach
swirling the seashells
dribbling onto the feather soft
sand patches between the rocks
exhaling it's mist

yet I knew
a quivering sea is hoarding a mighty power
steady and peaceful in its harnessed majesty
slumber yawning but doesn't fool me
when the sky starts moiling and roiling
and waves start to whimper
reckoning is coming
I start heading home
to avoid getting in the reach of harm's waves arms
when the sea gets angry

Angry Sea

my friend the fisherman
took me out to the sea one day
to help him test his new boat

the last escapade before winter's repose
I have always been yearning to experience the sea
right there in Poseidon's den

it was a dazzling mid-autumn day
a glowing circle of the chrome gold
breaking through the patches of
mackerel scaly plates
high in the stratosphere
below them cumulus puffs
gliding towards the horizon
hurried back and forth by the wheezing winds
feverish golds yellows oranges
bonfire red leaves
nudging us "move on
it's our time to shine now"

the riparian blue sea was groaning
ebb gasping waves running ashore
impatiently nodding the boat
approving tide's prompt arrival

soon after we left the harbour
waves started to whimper
bubbling and hissing
battering the rocky shore
growling in anger
hurtling the wave tops in its rage

suddenly the sky became abyssal black
a feral sea started spewing
its bruised bitterness
against anything on its way
had to cruise away
from this maniacal rage
onto open waters
the boat was sturdy and could easily weather
this suppurating hatred of the sea

wandered at sea aimlessly for a few hours
waiting for the roaring waves to unwind
as they say in my neck of the woods
if you don't like the weather
just wait for an hour

so finally sky started to cheer up
barbarous sea had spent itself
became humane again
we were so beholden to the nature
to let us come safely home
and of course
friend's boat has passed the test

_____

I don't use my eyes much, what I see is in my mind and in my
heart. And no punctuation to limit anyone's interpretation.
Allpoetry.com/Robert_Poleski

[Christophe Kristof Domšić]

Untitled

On the edge of the light in the shadow of reveries, the sun sets a
spiral of endless embers enlaying rainbow fires filled with madness
above the desert of the hills of my oblivion where the last
glimmers of the horizon flees the end of my fingers putting her
lips in a rain nourishing thousands of memories with a flowery
voice mixing with the mauve blue of my dull eyes watching the
stars fall at the end of life in the dark galleries of my insomnia that
pour out the black of a perfume of paradise donating my wrists
than I scarify ......

On the edge of the light in the shadow of reveries
the sun sets a spiral of endless embers
enlaying some rainbow fires filled with madness
above the desert of the hills of my oblivion
where the last glimmers of the horizon flees
the end of my fingers putting her lips in a rain
nourishing thousands of memories with a flowery voice
mixing with the mauve blue of my dull eyes
watching the stars fall at the end of life
in the dark galleries of my insomnia
that pour out the black of a perfume of paradise
donating my wrists than I scarify ......

Sur le bord de la lumière à l'ombre des rêveries
le soleil couche une spirale d'une braise infinie
incrustant des feux d'arcs en ciel emplis de folie
au-dessus du désert des collines de mes oublis
où les dernières lueurs de l'horizon fuit
le bout de mes doigts posés ses lèvres en une pluie
nourrissant milliers souvenirs d'une voix fleurie
se mélangeant au bleu mauve de mes yeux ternis
regardant tomber les étoiles d'une fin de vie
dans les galeries ténébreuses de mes insomnies
qui déversent le noir d'un parfum de paradis
faisant don de mes poignets que je scarifie.

My name is Chris, I'm living in Paris, France, here, on
alloetry.com, I'm writing since june, 2009 a story of love, natures,
personnal and sometimes, something dark in 150 grains of
melancholy. Allpoetry.com/Chris-Charmer

[R G Kaimal]

The Family

The family was a
circus.

Father once bought
talcum powder wholesale;
one thousand tins!
Emptied the bookcase to
store them.
Sold the books at the
second-hand market!

And one day
Mother made a jam which
after setting looked like
shampoo.

One day absentminded
father mistook it for one and
applied it liberally.

And then his peak
transformed rapidly.
Looked like
overripe papaya!

No specialist could
cure him.
Carried the
'papaya' head with him
for the rest of
his life!

_____

R G Kaimal has been writing since I was in school.
Storyhouse.org & Quantum Shorts have featured his short
stories. He is a regular contributor to AllPoetry.com. Over 2000
of his poems have been featured. Allpoetry.com/R.G.Kaimal

[Laura Sanders]

Penguins

Penguins- eighteen varieties, exist of this iconic bird,
living in forests, on snow sheets, coasts- noise most certainly
heard.
Flightless, webbed feet, compact with waterproof coats,
the sort of bird we all admire the most.

They thrive in crashing waves, and balance on rocks,
with black and white suits, huddling together in flocks.
In harshest places, this little chap hops,
relishing icy water, dives in with a flop!

Propels himself under water, with stretched out little wings,
makes those strange sounds, not like other birds, doesn't sing.
Like a little old man shuffling along,
beady eyes close, together they all throng.

In their dinner attire ,they look exquisitely dressed,
Penguins are so comical, it is the bird I like best.
My favourites are the Emperor, Adelie and Chinstrap,
fluffy youngsters toss their heads, as their mother nearby naps.....

————————————

I live in a beautiful part of England and I receive inspiration for
writing my poems , simply by walking and observing the
countryside throughout the year. I also enjoy observing people
and nature. Allpoetry.com/Laura_Sanders

[Joan Rooney]

Beit She'an

A splice of Heaven sits where
the Jordan and Jezreel meet
nestled below a tellurian Tel.

One column stands alone,
a composite capital
crowned with a crescent moon.

Rows of ancient ruins run
along a limestone road,
sounds of Roman chariots now stilled.

Rounded arches span above
a Nymphaeum font,
with hypocausts of Roman blasts.

A serpentine path rises behind
scaling a viridian hill,
iridescent in the Israeli sun.

I'm a retired librarian living in Ottawa Canada. I have done a lot
of genealogical research for myself and others. I am interested in
photography and I have written poems for over 25 years now.
Allpoetry.com/Joan_Rooney

[Kenneth Canatsey]

Five Days into Fall and the Weather's Fine

It's quiet here, backyard sounds of children playing
yield to a multi-chirping orchestra of happy sparrows -
and why not, the September weather's fine,
Fall's here, and though by afternoon they'll be silent
now the chit-chat's literally non-stop.
Our old oak's getting vaster, it needs trimming.
Susan wanted it cut down, but local law
says that's a no-no. Sometimes I think she's
secretly at war with nature, one bush and tree
at a time, trimmed branch by trimmed branch,
advancing death strategically like a frowning General.

Last year we said goodbye to the birch out front,
whose leaves she could never love when they fell
each fall and winter onto grass and gutter – what a mess!
The King Palm which replaced it looks sad and raggedy
with one big fan-leaf withered from tip to midriff.
That's what happens when you hire a tree trimmer to plant
a tree - no fertilizer gets thrown into the empty hole
and thus it's never thrived.

But now it's the simple sprinkler fork that captures my eye,
the smooth metal handle rusted to an elegant bronze
finish where the galvanizing's worn off due to
constant handling – worn clean as the palm of my hand,
its surface catches a glint of sunlight, and so

unobtrusive in its common beauty it's almost like
a Greco-Roman artifact in our local museum,
lying there for generations maybe
in a half-forgotten hall where no one ever visits.

Kenneth Canatsey lives in Agoura Hills CA with his wife of 33 years. His themes gravitate toward political satire, consequences of the pandemic, and the simple consolations of nature. Allpoetry.com/Kenneth.canatsey

[Bart Farmer]

It's Not My... I Can't Cry... If I Want To

One eye opens quicker than the other, so cute,
but who'll spearhead you home, me or the Neanderthal
host? Party goers head for the exit.
I seem to have sat down on a preset remote;
your laugh echoes the empty house mute.
White rain is a flat-screen,
crystalline-chilled, melting pixels.
Your other eye, I swear, winks at the storm.

A breaker, somewhere, thumbs a ride to the red zone.
Shadowy reflections of his indoor lighting
vanish from his TV
and abandon the glass of his aquarium.
Goldfish swim undisturbed
above the sediment of jagged, tiny stepping stones,
footholds for drunks to surface when bubbly

as with our host, brushing 'gainst you.
He toggles your dress by its fished out price
tag. Not my place to scan,
I blink like a readjusted lens off focus.

He sets us both out on the porch;
he's done with milking you to compliment him.
We're Banner milk bottles, side by side on the stairs.
Rain pelts milk-shiny, glassy sides. You shiver instead of going
numb and bottled up in reflections.

[Marilyn Griffin]

Shear Fun

her bleat pierces-
like whistling through
a thick blade of St. Augustine grass
high pitched and piteous
shrilling over the killing fields

of fleece sheared and
tangled in coils of wire
caught in our sweat
and in our lungs

rusted handpieces
still hang in the yard
near the wattle and daub shed-
babydoll faces now mute

a numbing of hook and grasp

Spring
they know the early sun
they know the tracings of earth
and moon,
the worn path

they know the shiver and blat
after the slideshoot-

spatchcocked
the nicks checked and released

and after,
the balm and salve of
their shepherd;

a reconciled cheer

Pines whispering haiku, goats in monotone bleating free verse,
lambs skipping through fields of nursery rhymes, my life is full of
words. Thank to Allpoetry for giving me a place to gather them!
Allpoetry.com/Greeningofautumn

[Howard Manser]

Aftermath

disco balls spin no more
confetti litters the floor

emerald-green bottles
knee-deep smother
an island incomplete

another day
nine to five
I survive capriciously alive

forestall
stop and stall
voyages devour my endless withering hours

the captain and crew are all aboard
my first mate is my adored
façade behind the mirage
I bid this party bon voyage

fractured reflections
hound
a maze-bound mouse

monstrous flashes warped and twisted
entwine

I find
not me or I

compost piles of rotting relics
the aftertaste
loiters past dawn

a bottom dweller
slithering
I crawled ashore
society followed building
on skeletons bleached and stored

spawned in a shallow tarn
from pond scum, I have grown
flowering, humanity failed
generations draped and veiled

granite records the hero
wood the last and least
anonymity commands no respect

Poetry is self-revelation. I am a son, brother, husband, father,
veteran, and poet hailing from the historic Golden Isles of
Georgia. I write my verse inspired by the seaside lifestyle.
Allpoetry.com/ProseAndCons

[Chelsea Rainford]

Difference of Night and Day

The salted sand is already burning
against my chapped finger-ends
and clapping palms

like this noontide sun
on the nape of my neck

as I wash the ocean clean
of weeds...

I'm gardening
in the sand and working my fingers
deep down to where
sea meets shore.

Coverall damp
and feet bare— standing,
bedraggled by nightfall

as my hair, salt-stiff and up-done
begins to mimic the garden hat
snatched
by a windy midday.

The sky watches,
its waning smile suspended
amongst a star-marked face

that breathes down
cool-breath breezes
and leaves sand and salt water
like ice.

_____

Chelsea Rainford grew up in suburbs along Lake Ontario, caught
between a chaotic city and dwindling farmland. That contrast,
combined with her unique perspective, expresses itself in all her
poetry. Allpoetry.com/C._E._Rainford

[Robert E. Ray]

Death of a Naturalist

after Seamus Heaney

All year the banks and dam
flanked by oaks and raspberry thickets
held the melt of winter, the rains
the algae, frogs, turtles and fish.
Truth: I am not a naturalist.

I catch-and-release—usually
because I am lazy
don't like to clean or cook
and I detest the aftertaste.
I like to dawdle by the lake

watch the minnows flicker
in the lightened shallows
the dragonflies levitate
reflecting the 6 o'clock sun
feel the sudden tug and drag

on the taut blue line
hear the old reel whine
the sunfish splash in the lilies
and tail-smack the soft mud.
The last catch was a keeper

but yellow-bellied, the only one
in the five-gallon bucket; puckered
lips bleeding, sucking up the hot air.
I looked down into her black eye

saw nothing.

She did not accept the clench
or the texture of my bare hand
or know how it would feel
to hit the flat brown water. I never
heard her scream or bawl

underwater. If I locked
the green gate off the dirt road
she might live
a full life of eleven years.
The average is eight

like marriage in America.
She is better off.

———————————

Robert E. Ray is a retired law enforcement officer and now serves
as a consultant. He lives in southeast Georgia.
Allpoetry.com/R.E._Ray

[Robert Poleski]

Dawn walk in the forest

almond-brown primeval forest
surrounds the small meadow
living near its edge
I enjoy morning's walks there
our creator's wake-up coffee

a winding moss-veiled trail
skirts the meadow
and heads to the pond-like lake
I can find it blindly
following the fragrance of
sweet woodruff along the path

the proud high-towering pines
stare me down
distrustful of my intentions
whisper and murmur
with gusts of wind cruising around
dropping in for a chat

a bespectacled sky is revealed
where the trees fall aside
the last of the morning's stars
glint like the silver pin pricks
an ore-gold moon in the distance
casts a honeyed sheen over the trees

an avian aria erupts
from the knot of trees ahead
the solitary song bird
starts pleading his pledge
join by the beaked consorts
creating a symphony of songs

idling past the suede soft flowers
ears perk up at metallic
tinkling sound of a stream
trees part and I see
it slides into the polished
silver mirror of an infinity pool

sit down relishing the moment
with back against the knobby boulder
head against the mossy pillow
close eyes and drift into infinity
let sweet fragrances
alluvial and palliative
etch in a memory for a while

—————————————

What I see is my own world, my whole intimate universe, with
my mind, my heart, looking inside things, inside feelings, what
makes it laugh or cry, love or hate, what makes it feel pleasure or
pain. Allpoetry.com/Robert_Poleski

[Marta E Green]

The Emerald Isle

A vivid alabaster full moon
rises above the hills and meadows
lunar eclipse has enchanted
the castle by the sea

oceans are calm
sailors are safe as the schooner the Andrea, drifts by
the captain guides the ship to the moorings in St. Martin
its shadow hovering on the sugary sandy beaches

iridescent blue lighthouse glows in the distance
bright shining yellow beacon
illuminates the shore

an artist captures the aquatic scene in a state of euphoria
sitting on the misty rocks by sea
using charcoal pencil sketching on stretched gessoed canvas

seeing the White Castle walls and windows
Duke of Arlington shows hospitality
rag tag sailors dance jigs
captain full in his cups, lets a jolly laugh roll out of his toothless
grin

Marta Green is from the state of Texas. She is passionate about family, animals, reading, art and especially writing poetry. Allpoetry.com/Marta_Green

[Christopher M Frangieh]
A Finches View

A baby finch no larger than a leaf
sprawls lovingly outside my window
seat; loud chirps shriek sharply
through its pointy beak with

squinty eyes darting back at me;
thin legs wobble across the tree
branch as it seeks out hot food
to slurp or eat; hobbling for the

worms poking up from the chipped
bark; claws clobber down on the
insects sprinting for safety from
this hungry infant.

———————————

Christopher M Frangieh was born in Boston MA and is a
Philosophical Poet. He believes nature is a friend
we can call on at anytime.
Allpoetry.com/Christopher_M_Frangieh

[Alicia Kish]
Daddy's Pills

tangled curls spread on the toilet seat
retching yellow fluorescent vomit
catlike scratches up and down her skinny adolescent arms
a balled-up t-shirt with blood on the bathroom floor
heaving so hard she's busted capillaries in her throat
choking on jack daniels and daddy's pills
her sister standing in the hallway crying
sirens blaze outside the house of horrors
yet another failed attempt

I am an artist a writer and most importantly a mother and wife. In
my free time, I travel as much as possible. There is nothing like
looking outside your own window into new worlds.
Allpoetry.com/Needtocreate

[Alwyn Barddylbach]

The Greenwood Gael

I snitch words from tips of branches,
sail close to troubled souls,
solar springs beneath my fingers,
wisps of greenwood gael.

Curry aloft on silver dale,
buried in mud-sea scrolls,
mountain dragons on stonewort walls,
townsfolk stalking trolls.

In stony brook, on purple fell,
over wollemi pine let's fly,
blackwood forest and cranky spell
our ordinance apply.

Oh eye of mind, my stomach pale,
quack of quail and shrew,
ghostly gum black lightning cry
on mountain cockatoo.

I snitch words from tips of branches,
sail close to troubled souls,
solar springs beneath my fingers,
wisps of greenwood gael.

In fairy falls the echo bluff,
the glen in autumn gown,
the tiger quoll on figs and lime,
funnel-web boast the crown.

Cattlefish markets, custard apples,
pinks mammoth orange pillow,
beastly *munchmallow* banksia men
feast on sunset willow.

Bearded dragon and eastern brown
fey slither through snowdrop's dew,
bold ginger skies in winter down,
great southern bight she blew.

We grieving sons and merry widows
entombed in brockworth abbey,
cox and hartley malting barley
moonshine in the belfry.

I snitch words from tips of branches,
sail close to troubled souls,
solar springs beneath my fingers,
wisps of greenwood gael.

My mother's bluebell lavender quill,
ink on springwood spray,
wasps and bees the heavens spill,
king parrots mellow fray.

Gangs of green and golden bell frog,
castle runes and blue-tongue twisters,
pot-bellied greenhood orchid trails
in violet redwood whispers.

Dead set ringers, cello and chime,
gumnut slingers shot through,
mass in cricket and summer rhyme
as waldron singers do.

Wattle and sunflower, saffron
glory star-bright yellow
glowing in labyrinth green,
west of woodford meadow.

Hakea and pink casuarina,
sweet rumble odelet brew,
pillars of the starry ether,
temples in mountains blue.

I snitch words from tips of branches,
sail close to troubled souls,
solar springs beneath my fingers,
wisps of greenwood gael.

––––––––––––

Kingdom of elves and poets, labyrinth green and temples blue,
garden of imagination - AB, Blue Mountains, New South Wales
Allpoetry.com/Barddylbach

[Paul Goetzinger]

Hot Springs

Hot springs
Mineral pools
Gurgle in isolation
Bathing spots
For relaxing
Dozens
Just off highways
Above rivers
Surrounded by views of mountaintops
Towering over ten thousand feet

Scattered in the hills
A spa for hikers
Dipping in the mud
Under a canopy of pine trees
Places for lumbermen and hippies
To simmer in a saucepan

Cascading down the side of a mountain
Hidden in the river canyons
Pouring from a cliff side cave
In the shade of cottonwoods and quaking aspen groves

While doves mingle in the shadows
Lured by little puffs of steam
Chipmunks steal a sack of trail mix left on a rock

Clouds rise towards a starry sky

Teasing silence

The wind in the trees

Fading

Into relaxation

Deep under the green ridges of forest jewels

———————————

Paul Goetzinger is a freelance writer and educator from Des Moines, Washington. He has been a writing articles for magazines and other publications for the past 17 years
Allpoetry.com/Paul_Goetzinger

[David E. Navarro]

Going Home

Sat in lecture hall rows of wooden chairs
surrounded by blank faces and
heard botanists speak of the perfect symmetry of flowers;
zoologists tell of the habits of wildlife and
the rituals they perform as families;
entomologists describe the social life of insects;
astronomers describe the formation of stars in nebulae;
and countless more professors drone on and on and on.
I read it, heard it, viewed slides and pictures—got good grades.

Graduated, I camped in the dark forest
surrounded by trees and underbrush and
inspected the perfect symmetry of a wisteria in bloom;
watched a beaver family build a hut and dam;
sat on a log full of fierce warring ants carrying off pupae;
leaned back at dusk and absorbed the brilliance of Orion,
the glow of its new stars forming, drawstrings on a pouch;
smelled pine, sassafras and false Solomon's seal;
ate choke cherries and wild black berries;
bled at the mercy of thorns and ran from the stench of the skunk.
I sniffed it, touched it, ate it, watched it—grades be damned—
I was home.

David E. Navarro is a poet-philosopher, author, essayist and
editor in Tucson AZ. Google/search 'David E. Navarro poet'
online for links and to learn more about his work.
Allpoetry.com/D.E._Navarro

[Diana Thoresen]

On Hidden Sophiologies of White Cockatoos

What strange hierophantic picture language do such heavenly
creatures speak?

Which celestial abode birthed your dazzling white magnificence?

Do landscape angels send you on my way with a missive every
evening?

Have you glanced hidden temples of light within jungle lianas and
fruit dove sanctuaries?

Is it you who helps the fledgling paradise kingfisher find its way
home to New Guinea?

Your delicate wings brushed aside the sugar factory canopies of
glossy rainforest leaves, ever hungry for the sun.

You've shed grace on the cruelties of nature and sang to the
strangler figs slowly suffocating a living tree in its vampire
embrace.

The sacred architecture of the forest with its Gothic sun ray
seeking spires is an open book to you.

You saw the Rainbow Serpent sacrifice himself in the Barron Falls
and become an ever living presence in every steep granite gorge
and soothing freshwater creek.

What of your Nemesis? Devil Birds? Black Cockatoos? Appalling and discursive epistemes, they weave their dark magic into the Meissen porcelain of dainty seashore shells.

No creature or landscape invisible shrine is ever at odds with the Earth's visionary geography:

We walk through the onion skin of sacred sites into the stars.

Diana Thoresen is a writer involved in free energy research. She's currently working on publishing "Donbass Chronicles: Dawid Hudziec Photography," a rare gem of photojournalism. Allpoetry.com/Diana_Thoresen

[Diana Thoresen]

A Black Wedding Dress

It was Bastille Day, July 14
Your childlike outpouring of joy, your dapper black suit
My hideous black crow of a dress
With your Robespierre tie
It was a last minute whim, like dipping
A Missoni handkerchief in royal blood

Something always survives
A relic, a bone, old cast iron gates
A prism of another self, fractured in a hundred
Mirror worlds and light coming in through a myriad of
Luminous pain butterflies
We summoned Pan, Lucifer, Mercury

In the lush mixed conifer forests
Something was weaving a dark dream beneath
All July meadow flowers and giant Douglas-firs
Lupines were a threat we never recognized
Mount Hood was seething with the rage of ancient pines
Transfixed, we watched a coyote sneak out of the mists

Tall grass, volcanic lava, and ash
His eyes were brimming with liquid gold
My God, the splendors of that land
You put me to sleep in a volcano land crypt

You conjured a sibyl out of the embers of the dazzling
White mountains

A glimpse of the eagles
A sanctifying smell of sagebrush is
All that remains of your wilderness seeping
Into my raspberry rhodochrosite blood
That house, that madness, that pain

Diana Thoresen is a writer currently living in Palm Cove,
Australia. She's fascinated by free energy research, photography
and metaphysics. Allpoetry.com/Diana_Thoresen

[Rick Warrior]

Plow/Shares

So I'm watching the Grocer
Stacking his Fruits and Vegetables
Lining up the Asparagus Spears
(In nice little Ice-Bed Rows)
Broccoli Crowns look up to The Sky
Carrot Parallelograms
Grapes Baggily Bunch
Pyramids of Oranges/Lemons/Limes/Yellow/Green
Sculptured Banana Fountains
And I'm thinking
Humans
"The Cream Lumpers" Species
Treat every other Species
Like it was in the whey

Rick was born in New Brunswick, Canada, the middle child of five. He held a variety of interesting jobs in the private and public sector. Allpoetry.com/RickthePoetWarrior

[Alicia Kish]

Jerrod

green wet blades of grass
Picasso's sharp-angled hill
locust buzzing their symphony
white diamonds twinkling
quadruple adolescent swing set
see-saw pitched
echoes of laughter
filling cool crisp night air
freckles, red hair
anxious mummers
bodies lean like broken trees
we wrap our branches

lips touch
lighting

wet mouths
hands
exhale

_____

I am an artist a writer and most importantly a mother and wife. In
my free time, I travel as much as possible. There is nothing like
looking outside of your own window to experience something
else. Allpoetry.com/Needtocreate

[Kelle Harrison]

Memories of Country Fields

Favorite memories of childhood
summer sun burns down
lingering, on the wheel well
Grandpa's old orange tractor
his denim clad knees beside me.
Riding high through the fields
wheat and corn grow.

Times with cousins and sister.
Cracking walnuts for Grandma
shucking corn for the pigs.
Climbing in the hayloft
Looking down at the farm.
Pigs in the pens, cows in the pasture
chickens cluck in the yard

Watching Grandpa cutting wood
load his old wagon with logs
ride on tractor back home.
His coveralls smell of oil and soil,
I didn't care for wood air mixed in.
Gates close, bang and clang lock
Keeping the cows wandering out.

One morning Grandpa came in
come with me little lady, I need you

gate left open, two cows loose,
running around the cornfield.
Chasing the heifers brown hide
whooping, yelling top of our lungs
return the cows to fields of clover.

Grandpa's been gone over thirty years
but the memories of days in the fields
will always remain the best time ever.

_____

I'm not always inspired to write, but when I am, my mind gets
jammed up with ideas. Hi, I'm Kelle from a little country town in
North East Ohio. My late husband was Aussie, my biggest fan,
inspired me Allpoetry.com/Kelsmiles

[Albert Keith Clement]

come on in, sit as I spin a tale

Garden City

a picturesque community where snails dwell
overlaid various variations of greenery
amidst fresh fragile flourishing flowers

careful, don't step in the slime trail
behind the mayor and his wife
handsome Dale and lovely Gale
they're Giant Land Snails

steadily sliding along next to them
Martingale and Monorail adopted
twin African snails - Berail and Derail

you must know while you're here
there is something we all fear
the owner of Frenchies Bistro
Sinister Mister French Stench

and his Wicked Chef, Chaff
setting traps taking our friends
serving them in his specialty
unique garlic broiled escargot

yesterday two-families disappeared
brothers Tweed and Tweedle

there little sister Dovetail
dad Bobtail, mom Ponytail

and a group of friends
Ale, Brail, Bewail, and Borrell
none of them to be seen again
unless you ate Chaff's Specialty

In my youthful years, I was a Venturous Wondering
Misanthrope. I hitchhiked across Edmonton, Calgary, and
Vancouver. I sojourned along the Coast Highway and relaxed on
the white sandy seashores. Allpoetry.com/Postilion

[Kristof Domšić]

The mystery of the world

A dazzling reflection gilds my skin. I'm over there, on the edge of
the water. But today I am not going to take a bath. I will go in the
shade of my pages telling her the story of a woman who
offered me the fame of my love. I am there, alone on the sand, I
bought myself the sea.

Do you see the sea dancing ?
It's like living with the ocean,

... the waves as in the hollow of the sheets ...

Trom dark to black would come in the evening
and in the first diamonds of a dust
randomly a fragment of moon would light up

... the dreams of the heavens as in the open ...

and nothing would be a sanctuary anymore
stars and flowers will grow, bloom
so we can stay together
balanced around the infinite mystery of a "bubble"

I love the ocean ... Cradled around you ... And I, alone to go
around the world ... I will watch you go ... Afraid to be forgotten
by this heartache that should to be just for both of us ...
I look at myself in the mirror...
I imagine myself asleep under the sand ...

A smile on her lips ... The flux...

Divine sun on your nail ... The tingling ... The sight creates the
sound ... The color is only a reflection ...

Emotion does the rest ...

She has no words ...

I run like a tree ...

Turning, turning around the cosmic waves ...

Reverence ... Prayer ... Sacred fire ...

I owe him the sacrifice ...

The lands are only toys ... The filaments? ... Let! ... You would
not understand! ...

*Un éblouissant reflet dore ma peau. Je suis là-bas, au bord de
l'eau. Mais aujourd'hui je n'irai pas prendre de bain. J'irai à
l'ombre de mes pages la racontant. L'histoire d'une femme qui m'a
offert la célébrité de mon amour. Je suis là-bas, seul sur le sable. Je
me suis acheté la mer*

Le Mystere du Monde

Vous voyez danser la mer ?
c'est comme vivre avec l'océan...

... Les flots comme au creux des draps ...

du sombre au noir viendrait le soir
et dans les premiers diamants d'une poussière
au hasard d'un éclat s'illuminerait un fragment de lune

... Les songes des cieux comme à ciel ouvert ...

et plus rien ne serait un sanctuaire
étoiles et fleurs grandiront, fleuriront
afin que nous puissions rester ensemble
en équilibre autour du mystère infini d'une « bulle »

J'aime l'océan... Bercé autour de vous... Et moi, seul à faire le tour
du monde... Je vous regarderai partir... Apeuré d'être oublié par ce
chagrin d'amour qui ne devait être rien que pour nous deux...
Je me regarde dans le miroir...
Je m'imagine endormi sous le sable...
Le sourire aux lèvres... L'Écoulement...
Soleil divin sur votre ongle... Le tintement... La vue créée le son...
La couleur n'est qu'un reflet...
L'émotion fait le reste...
Elle n'a pas de mot...
Je cours tel un arbre...
Tournant, tournant autour des flots cosmiques...
La révérence... La prière... Le feu sacré...
Je lui dois le sacrifice...
Les terres ne sont que des jouets... Les filaments ?... Laissez
!...Vous ne comprendriez pas !...

My name is Chris, I'm living in Paris, France, here, on
alloetry.com, I'm writing since je is 2, a story of love, natures,
personnal and sometimes, something dark in 150 grains of
melancholy. Allpoetry.com/Chris-Charmer

[Ropani Sebit Simbe]

Dreams

Her mind is filled with thoughts, caged and unfiltered
With so much sensual dreams you're unforgettable
Whisper intimate words that make my body quiver
Move your hands in between my legs as I lie and watch your
fingers dance for me.

Her body laid still as she watched him above
Eyes deep, black as night, breathing heavy, trying to concentrate.
His tongue painted her body as he listened to her moan

Su piel magnética, lo acerca
Ojos encerrados de nuevo
Le dice a él que no pare
Él no para
Es demasiado intenso, tanto la química sobre el poder de la
habitación
Los moranos y los gemidos se hacen más fuertes
Llegó a su fin y todo lo que oyes es silencio y respiración pesada

––––––––––––––––––

My name is Ropani. Im young writer from New York City, NY. I enjoy all poetry because it helps me develop as a better poetry writer and the feedback I get from the community is outstanding! Allpoetry.com/Ropani

[Annette Gagliardi]

Mass Transit

I chose public transport
To view the ebb and flow of humanity -
To check the tide-pool of San Fran;
The going in and going out - the in and out and in and out.

The burl-lipped homeless, whose coat drip with eons of street
diligence -
happy to have a seat to breath the paying-customer air,
going nowhere more quickly than the endless shuffle of days gone
by.
Going in and going out; and in and out, and in and out.

Aged career girls with slashed, lip-sticked mouths
who arch and flex on dancer legs that swim inside their little girl
clothes;
and wear their self-possessed assurance like hats over well-
manicured
heads that flaunt the going in and going out, going in and going
out.

Tiny Chinese ancients mumble incantations
and gum invisible vittles with toothless mouths;
with walking sticks that tap a three-legged rhythm as they
shuffle on and off, going in and out, and in and out.

Step lively, now. Sit and sway. Stand in honor
of those less fortunate and gaze sideways
at their maladies without conscious contempt or pity.
Watch their going in and going out and in and out and in and
out.

Annette Gagliardi, who is from Minneapolis, Minnesota has self-published two poetry books titled: "Life Prints: A Collection" and "Reflections of Sunshine". See more at: annettegagliardi.com Allpoetry.com/Annette45

[Randall Reedy]

The Taste of an Olive

O' for the taste of an olive
speared by a toothpick, floating
aloft in vermouth

I make a toast to beauty
as swizzle stick memories stir
care free days of youth

maiden voyages of vessels
toasting absinth over ice
when the glacier hits the Titanic

we are unsinkable ships
you crash into me, like a cresting wave
splashing across my bow

as we lose ourselves
in the taste of green, glycerin
slow kiss upon virgin lips

iceberg ahead
whiskey and bourbon on jagged shores
consoling maritime daydreaming

O' for the taste of an olive
speared by a tooth pick, floating
aloft in vermouth

The man behind the mask, that is the villain known as Papa Terminus, I like to experiment with poetic structures and styles...this allows me to stay fresh and new
Allpoetry.com/Papa_Terminus

[Marilyn Griffin]

the blues and the grays

Over this saturated field the eagles roam
hooded eyes search for carrion from the shadowed nooks
over the ground the squirrels scurry from sight
over the blues and over the grays
soldiers in soft repose; their bodies a final closure in grave sleep

wildflowers unfold in perfumed layers of spring
can no one remember these who lie here
under showers
under letters tucked in pockets of moss
under branches that catch a ray of sun and point the way?
rusted weapons that fell with brothers and sons
farmers who walked away with empty sockets and
pulled frayed photos from pocked coats to the snap of
drum and boot (the snap of the leg or neck)

they lay under leaves that gather and fall
oh gather together mothers and fathers
gather these sons and heave your arms high
carry him to a deeper grave and do not let
these phantoms of seasons cover
what you have forgotten-
waiting for your own to come home

Sometimes my thoughts go to places I've never been, to time zones where I haven't existed. Thank you to Kevin and allpoetry for letting me explore and to cast lines to see if I get any bites.
Allpoetry.com/Greeningofautumn

[Lewis E. Waxman]

The treatment

Forty five days irradiating a walnut size organ
stumbling from bed to urinal relentlessly
burning bowls, irritated rectal palps, bleeding red
staying alive urged the song over again in my head.

Aiming at ten years more signaled by PSA near zero.
unknown waiting negligible reacting
three months to two years
days to be filled with other issues of more urgent sustainability
hour glasses sand shifts and another cell hits the dust.
Not so bad.

———————————

I began writing poems on rainy nights in Kenya in 1967. Over the
years I have focus on having something to say. Hopefully, I have
been heard. I have over 100 poems on the Allpoetry.com site.
Allpoetry.com/LEW

[Joan C. Fingon]

Dreams of the Cove

he dreams about being
in the south end of the cove
hearing a red-wing blackbird trill
paddling in his kayak
through light feathery reeds
in the early morning mist

gliding along the shoreline
silently dips his paddle
into the salty waters
in a natural rhythm

within the silvery reeds
he settles into a spot facing east
watching yellow and cinnamon colored streaks
the silhouette of a white crane flying
low across the horizon

———————————

Joan loves with her cat and husband in sunny Ventura. When she
is not gardening she is reading or writing poetry.
Allpoetry.com/Poetry_lover7

[Ryan Hunt]

[the sky is blue and filled with blue]

the sky is blue and filled with blue
the blue is beyond itself
through the blue I descend to the meadow
where blue bells ring in the spring
sounding their triumph in the buzzing bees

those bees occupying the secret sex
of flower upon flower
petals, pistils, stamens yielding fortunate
nectar to be lapped and bundled
brought back to the hive through the blue

where honey is profited and rendered
to the queen in all her dancing glory
signaling the spread of life unheard
undanced and undone
her followers holding close and bringing
news of the sky and blue she no longer
sees either by day or by night

still, in the night she hears the moon
from inside her hive and she whispers
to the moon her deepest secrets hidden
far from the hive and deep in her heart
the secret that she knows her longing

for the sky and the blue are the part
of her dance revealing the blue within her

she spins that whisper to the moon
those two sisters of the stars
remember each other in the night

when I wake in the morning
rising with the sun shining in the window
I spread sweet cream butter on my bread
lather thick the honey
in every bite I hear the queen
whisper to moon of the sky and blue
looking up I see their secret
and I know it is my secret too

———————————

Ryan lives in Berkeley, California where he watches the sun set over the Golden Gate Bridge and scratches out poetry on scraps of paper and phone screens indiscriminately.
Allpoetry.com/Ryan_Hunt

[Christopher M Frangieh]

The Ocean In Me

Paper never looked and
smelled so good; like an
ocean of thin waves with

blue lines sliding across
my page. I lean my arm
down for a touch from

the sea's cold hand; I
sit by her and gaze
at the sailing clouds

drifting above the
oceans sparkling
face. I reach for

my pen as a red
winged blackbird
pushes their beak

through sand for
leftovers by the
army of marching

crabs, forming in
bands by the shore;
pink jellyfish float to

the surface for a look
at the deep mind bathing
in the depths of a fast

moving age; the one to
dive in without knowing
how to swim or say help

for my own sake of being;
here on the edge where
other poets go missing.

Christopher M. Frangieh is from Massachusetts and has practiced
the art of writing poetry since he was an adolescent. He considers
his writing style as Philosophical.
Allpoetry.com/Christopher_M_Frangieh

[Lorri Ventura]

Paupers Cemetery

Turkey vultures
Venture beyond a nearby landfill
Circling evocatively above the paupers' graves
On Mayflower Hill.

Grave markers resemble key heads
Bearing not names, but numerals
A potter's field
Stretching from a trash-strewn roadside to a forest

Unnamed graves embrace the insane
Forced to sew their own burial shrouds
While hunched on cots
In the nearby state hospital

Alongside them are infants and children
Resting eternally with strangers
In group plots
To conserve space

The earth comforts the nameless poor
Their dreams curtailed by monsters
Bearing melodic names—
Diphtheria, Dropsy, Dysentery, Dementia, Despair

Beneath numbered iron markers
Lie the forgotten, abandoned, and lost
Lives perhaps un-noted
But not without value

Lorri Ventura is a retired special education administrator living in Massachusetts. Her writing has been featured in several anthologies. Allpoetry.com/Lorri_Ventura

[Arlice Davenport]

Whale Songs

Like Leviathan of old,
the rough, angry ocean
pummels the basalt shore
and its denizens of the deep.

California grey whales
breach the surface of
the autumnal Oregon waters, slide
over the waves like seals
on a hunt,
their colors mingle perfectly
with the yellow-tinged whitecaps,
their bodies aimed
perfectly south.

How innocent they sound
as their songs penetrate
the cacophony of the
crashing surf.

How magnificent they sound;
untranslated poetry, haunting
love lyrics, caressing
the beloved with a sonata
of sonar.

Like a child, they sing for joy,
and the sea turns a deaf ear.

But I hear them, and am transfixed
by their emotion and intelligence.
They sing to me, a mammalian
serenade at dusk.

I dare not sing back
for fear of failure. Of foolishness.

Yet I weep to hear them sing again,
once more, before their majestic
passing to the milder seas of Mexico.

———————————————

Oregon's coast is magical, full of beauty and power. The presence
of grey whales raised the intensity level to the ecstatic. With their
cries, the whales sounded almost human. I gave them wide berth.
Allpoetry.com/arliced

[Bobbie Breden]

Vernal Awakenings

Heaven on earth awakens
Burgeoning patches of utopia
Emerald fingers ascend
From beneath dusky cloaks of mulch

Tender bright blades of jade
Materialize from between
Brittle funereal remnants of the previous summer
Drab corpses protect determined new shoots

Daffodils, jonquils, narcissus,
Pronounce seasonal change
Fragrant hyacinths' perfume
Greet the eager gardener

Trees veiled in chartreuse
The woods home to quiet magic
Timber donning their verdant mantle
Hinting at imminent lush summer foliage

Enveloped in a feathered serenade
Birds offer triumphant song
Heralding their victory
Winter endured and vanquished

Back deck my private Shangri-la
Windchimes jingling the eupnoea of spring
Unite in their own atonal chorus
Balmy breeze making blithesome music

Apperceive the cyclical rebirth
Rejuvenation unfolds, amplifies
The bedecked earth celebrates
A resonant vibrant festival

Retired Lady Leatherneck (US Marine), Renaissance woman, and
a lover of life's mysteries. I'm interested in how others view the
universe, and welcome opportunities to see it through their eyes.
Allpoetry.com/Captain_B2

[Stephan V. Mastison]

The Fog

A Murder Mystery

Night like a shroud, blankets the sand and the sea.

In the distance a rolling fog clings to the tide.

The fog is like a living thing as it enters the harbor.

It Swallows up the ships into a gray abyss

As it inches toward the shore.

One lone fisherman ignores the threat

And just continues to fix his nets.

The fog now reaches the coast

The ancient mariner stands his ground.

For an instant the two enemies meet

The fog advances the man will not retreat.

The man vanishes in the ghostly mist.

Like an army, the fog maneuvers over the coastal plane.

Retreating as daybreak begins.

Slowly returning to the sea.

Past the point where the fisherman made his final stand.

A silent reminder of the mystery and of the man.

———————————

My name is Stephan V. Mastison and I am a published author with two books They are 'Shadows in the Mist' and 'Crossroads, and the journey home'. My hope is to inspire and be thought provoking. Allpoetry.com/S.V._Mastison

[Joan Rooney]

Mount Tabor

An ancient round-arched Romanesque shrine
a church perched high upon a hill,
resting atop old crusader stones
upon a crumbling Byzantine wall,
a memorial to illumine a site,
where Heaven and earth did once meet.

Carefully-constructed windows beam
rays of golden, glistening sunlight
transfiguring and trans-illumining,
a domed apse of gleaming mosaic
where Jesus, Moses, and Elijah stand resplendent
in reverent, iridescent light.

Souls transport to a much higher plane,
hearts fly to a distant dimension,
while astonished apostles cower below
James, Peter and John struck with awe,
when a voice calls through the marble walls,
"this is My Son with whom I am well-pleased".

———————————

I'm a retired librarian living in Ottawa Canada. I have done a lot
of genealogical research for myself and others. I am interested in
photography and I have written poems for over 25 years now.
Allpoetry.com/Joan_Rooney

[David I Mayerhoff]

Night of Make-Believe and Real

I lunge ahead
onto the street called Bourbon
masked party- goers fiddling their
satin costumes and curled whiskers

passing all teeth
biting while grinding
blood dripping from the
TMJ of the gargoyle

sounds curdling the stomach,
stink to fill a dumpster
knives jutting out
in place of nails

the half naked
less scary than the clothed
in their skin of decay
weeping corpuscles of red
and pus of green

fangs ripping at flesh
of the beast newly killed
with cackling to stand the hair
on the head of the bald

goblins rocking to music
of the netherworld
as if on drugs

a night under the stars
with the moon
acting as friend and foe
shining on predator and prey

the gleam on my eye moist
as if I was shouting 'outta here'
when I discover
this is all too real
and the exits lead me
deeper inside

David I Mayerhoff is an emerging literary writer, an established scientific author, and a Clinical Professor of Psychiatry. He grew up on Long Island and now resides in New Jersey. Allpoetry.com/David_Mayerhoff

[Jennifer D English]

A Hundred Forms of Fear

Driven by this
they say
I am afraid
so
if it were so
you may gather them like flower

a bouquet of answered prayers
and relentless dreamers
would fit under

ribbon
gentle when they pull
pink bow around
succulent stems

no thorns here
no nips to draw blood
no tears to wet cheeks

we
are
resting
on laurels like children
faces down

it's been long since
any have seen horizon
changing color from a setting sun
or a rising one

for pinks and purples
for yellows and oranges
strike chords in blue

now sad eyes look away
aches melodically dance
through my repressed body
where night brings the only
comfort any of us
have ever known.

———————————

I am what I would call a 'Dark Poet'. I've always been drawn to the hurt and broken. Maybe because I am one. Poetry for me is healing. Maybe if one person reads something I write, then can relate and not feel so alone, I've done my job as a poet.
Allpoetry.com/JensGoneMad

[Annette Gagliardi]

Old Hotel

Camphor predominantly persists
in the air as I stroll the large
hospital ward checking on pulse and pressure.

Injured men lie in tethered rows of beds —
some moaning, some sighing
others lying still.

Loneliness lingers long in the hallways,
listening and waiting like a dawdling school boy,
melding well with bed sheets and band aids.

It sneaks like scurrying rat feet about an old hotel,
pilfering strength, nibbling the crusts
of courage remaining

that hide in sight of the light shining
in through the south windows,
providing a port in this winter's storm.

Affliction lists leeward and slyly
saps strength from souls
lingering or departing.

Annette Gagliardi has poetry published in the Southwest Journal, Dreamers Creative Writing Online, Down in the Dirt Online Magazine, Trouble Among the Stars, Poetry Quarterly, Poetic Bond and others. Allpoetry.com/Annette45

[Tina Thrower]

Nature

I lie awake in the early morning dew as frost awakens the nearby
forest animals....
Deer, Squirrels, Birds, Rabbits,
Afar from them you hear and see the gushing water of the
waterfall as it babbles over the golden brook.....
how pretty to see the flowing water aimlessly....
misty waters in the neverlands along the shady trees Nottingham
forest

––––––––––––––––––––

My World: I'm a mother and grandma, I love the great outdoors,
bowling, watching movies and going on walks. I'm mainly just
trying to live one day at a time. Allpoetry.com/Icygreenleopard4

[Esteban Barnes]

Sunflowers

Golden bows stem from hazelnut eyes
that glare silently as the sun sprays light:
making weeds envy their golden locks
and butterflies dance around their petals, giving smiles
to the passersby in the sweet glow of summer.

I am an English teacher from Lima, Peru, who enjoys reading, writing and drawing creative inspiration from existing authors, as well as the many things in life (and person) that I love. Allpoetry.com/Barnesy

[Jeanette Showalter]

After The Party

The last guests bid their fond goodbyes.
I barricade the door and sigh.
The party scored a fine success:
(one complaint and no arrests).

Judging by this happy mess,
of tangled pillows, rumpled chairs,
crepe paper drooping everywhere.
Party perfume No. 9:
cigars, stale beer, and carton wine.

Balloons tip toe across the floor.
(They shall float, ah, nevermore).
Paper plates and plastic forks
lie obsolete as champagne corks.

Beneath my feet the carpet crunches;
(munchies for tomorrow's lunches).
An orphaned coat drapes on the chair.
A hat droops from the chandelier.

The dog is scarfing chips and cake.
He knows I won't be long awake.
I don't think I can climb the stairs,
(and who knows what I'll find up there).
I'll curl up in the nearest chair.

The cuckoo's door is soundly blocked.
The TV's off, the front door's locked.
Tomorrow I will clean this mess.
tonight I need to get some...

"zzzzzzzzzz"

Jaye is a writer in San Diego, CA and enjoys researching facts for her poetry and magazine articles. Writing is a learning tool that is relaxing, distracting, and creative. Allpoetry.com/Jaye_Showalter

[Manda Martinez]

Summer

A day full of running wild and skinned knees
Frogs and lizards, butterflies and bubble bees
The night full of stars, lightning bugs, and a breeze
Thunderstorm whips the wind through the trees

I usually just write what comes to me. I've always loved writing.
It's always been a passion of mine. I wrote a poem in sixth grade
that my librarian kept in the library to read every year.
Allpoetry.com/Lovable_Sunrise

[Hunter Aydelott]

Determined Chins

"chins up" always the expression
as a matter of strict principle
laughing in the face of doubt
smiles radiance reassuring

worries stomped by strides forward
seeking the suns warm embrace
marching in a generals brass band
break dancing with ease and grace

or like captains ocean silhouette
against a moonbeams shadow
the rugged determined pipe smoke
contemplating waters fathom

true grit erasing palpations
gut wrenching and relentless
the drive that decries greatness
steadfast against the wind bending

I live in Cypress Texas. I'm a rescue diver that loves underwater
photography. I also play keyboard in my friends garage band and
have amassed a large music collection. Another hobby is mosaics.
Allpoetry.com/Burnside

[James C Gammie]

Come to Long Island

It's almost silent / but for the echoes of Jack Teagarden's honeyed call / and a maid hushing stragglers / as she fishes Highball flutes from the pool

Is it Springtime? / It's hard to see the sun / above Long Island's vaulting ambition

I roll this way and that in choppy sheets / until I notice him / the finest silhouette in Sands Point

Hunkered down I study him / partially immersed in emerald drapes / he sucks all the goodness from a Chesterfield / before expelling his pickled woes in a cloudy bellow

The party? / well / from what I remember / there were girls and boys and far too much noise / so I hid in his half-smiles / and searched for him in his faraway looks

The girls are shameless these days / really / full of high-proof liquor and unbuttoned morals / Dana says it's a wonder he notices me at all / but he does / he always does

I leave the safety of the sheets and slide in behind him / wrapping my arms around an empire / one built on the back of others / that's propelled us towards the limits of credulity

The garden / littered with throw away indulgences / leaks into the ocean / the only thing he's yet to own

He turns and warms me with attention / before explaining he'll be out for a night / maybe two / deals to be cut in the city and all

The phone rings / the tempo changes / and he's gone / swapping sounds / with a thief at the other end of the line

You know / every time he sees me / I lose something / like the sandy-haired girl on the shores of Dare County / dimes slipping like sand through my excited fingers at the Fair / and he loses something too / maybe his pretence of patience

It's quarter past something / so I fold myself back into bed / without him the day is lost

Roll on summer / when we'll jump off Salisbury Creek at night / smashing the milky cymbal beneath our feet / I'm sure every girl wants to live till summer

_____

Lives happily on the South Coast of England with wife and two daughters. James has enjoyed reading and writing poetry from an early age. Allpoetry.com/James_Vasenco

[Eugenia Fain]

Christmas Season

Candy canes and Christmas stockings
Hung by blazing fires,
Christmas tunes played on harp and lyre,
Christmas caroling in the neighborhood,
And noble firs brought from the woods,
Halls decked with boughs of holly,
Bell ringers and Santa, oh so jolly,
Presents underneath the fir,
Like the gifts of gold, frankincense and myrrh,
Christmas morn, a jubilant time
Of celebrating the Savior's birth
So very sublime.

———————————

Mywife304@aol.com resides in Columbia, SC with her husband
Ivan and cat Buddy. She is an English major from Duke
University (1991), Eugenia has published since age eleven.
Allpoetry.com/Mywife304

[S. Libellule]

Le Jardin Poetique

It is the perfect place to play
then write the day away
within ivy trellised nooks
beneath a true cerulean blue

With nothing left to do
but pluck plump words
ripe off the vine
before pearling them on a line

I find each poem
a new home
I lose track of all time
riding a wave of soft rhyme

———————————

From Alabama, Libellule enjoys reading and writing poetry. Strongly influenced by ee cummings and Mary Oliver, Libellule's poetry is introspective with a deep reverence for language and the everyday Allpoetry.com/LilDragonFly

[Joan Fingon]

A Touch of Innocence

just thirteen
laughing and racing
together to their favorite
old oak tree
in the nearby field

out of breath
tumbling together
under the shady tree
they laugh

he leans in
for that first kiss
lips touch lips
surprising each other
in the mid afternoon sun

_____

Joan Fingon lives in Ventura, California with her husband and
cat. She spends time in her back garden writing poetry.
Allpoetry.com/Poetry_lover7

[Ken Makepeace]

Autumn Leaves

Autumn leaves, heavy
under foot
Horse chestnuts falling
to the ground.

Dark nights creeping in
Street lights all aglow
People rushing to be near
the fire.

This is the autumn I know
so well, cold and bleak and
not so meek.

Now all we need is some
snow to complete this
autumnal show.

———————————

Makepeaceken is from North Wales, in the UK, where I have
lived most of my life. I took up writing after going on coyrse at a
local college when I was in my mid forties
Allpoetry.com/LonePoet

[Audrey Kinler]

her pearl eyes

those rims
of a wine glass
were smothered
in marks from her
the edges of her own
incandescent lipstick
with a glossy soft hint
her signature was Angie
but her name was Angela
with her beady blue pearls
for eyes, a phantom dress
and a gauzy glass of fizzy
champagne, quite fruity
and delightfully sweet
her glass clicked to
the sound of my
shrill, hoarse
whines
my whine
shook her
she covered
her ears from
the screams of
shrill, uncomfort
shriek, that was an

accident on my part, I
forgot my noises were
to be constantly shunned
what a humungous forg I am
but she opened her eyes
of iridescent blues, and
held out her warm hand
when I took her hand
we walked away
to the waning,
summer
sunrise
me
and the
girl in the
phantomly
dress and the
glass of alcohol
that fizzes into
a soft foam that
sweetens while I
shows her the
way past
living

————————————

Audrey is from New Orleans. Her interest in poetry started at a young age and has sprouted since. She writes poems in her free time on allpoetry.com. Allpoetry.com/TrueArtistmations

[Subha Rajesh]

Alone in his moods

he was all of darkness made
silent and brooding
opaque and still
in the dark he stood
not a whisper heard
his silver streaks unseen

ominous silence unnerving
a mysterious aura conquers
unflinching stare
emotions held in check
silent anger a fear
whirls ready to ensnare
his unforeseen temper tides
stood apart
nerves taut

not even a silhouette
on this uncanny night
no grace from the moon
only a wink of an apathetic star
couldn't hear him breathe
do stormy days ahead of him
cause this squeamish prequel
untenable conflicts bombard
reached out in sorrow now mine

inexplicably entwined in his net
cobwebs invisible surround

alone in his moods
no breeze as console
a tender caress of its beloved fingers
to render life on a nocturne's quiet
one sketch painted black
hugging the horizon
ocean merged

awaiting a turn
I persevere
leaning on time

the morning after he will dawn
sparkling and vivid
when curious smiles arise
with a darling sun's touch
his waves shall reach out to me
a rendezvous by bridging panes
beatific morning
before the turbulence in the city
drown our voices
we shall greet
and go on with our lives

―――――――――

Subha Rajesh is from India. She takes inspiration from nature,
life, and humanity. The constant support from her beloved
family has helped her take off on this poetic journey.
Allpoetry.com/Bluewrite76

[Arlice W. Davenport]

Love Immemorial

The poverty of memory blanches
all objects of desire. Events gurgle up
from an unconscious soup, evanescent
as bubbles in a fine champagne,
diligent as cells churning blood into oxygen.
I recall our clinging to each other,
the first kiss an interlocking piece
of the sexual puzzle that forever lacks
the solution's final fragment.

Love plays with matches
in the winter wind. Remembrance
whisks past, pressed to avoid
the cost of recreating what is only
ghostly, of swinging on naked branches
to materialize as mind. O how the past
sucks the marrow from our bones,
leaving limp limbs, parallel thumbs.
How we yearn for substance,
for a love immemorial, a lasting
kiss *sans* mound or stone.

Love is the bottomless topic of so much poetry around the globe.
It is elusive and certain at once, fulfilling and frustrating. Time is
the culprit, ensuring that the present joy we find never lasts
Allpoetry.com/arliced

[Marta E Green]

Innocence, Out of the Mouth of Babes

I'm a young thirteen year old girl,
with long black hair and chocolate eyes
hanging out with a Rusty with vivid blue eyes, of the same age
who is dressed in brown shorts and a black AC/DC t-shirt
playing truth or dare

he chooses dare
putting his hand on my face
and kisses me with the softest lips
tongue, patient and teasing

my emotions are like a roller coaster
climbing up on wooden tracks and then free falling down
I am giddy with excitement
a first kiss by an experienced boy
I hide my emotions so my family won't know

_____

Marta Green is from the great state Texas. She loves nature, writing, reading and spending time with her family! Allpoetry.com/Marta_Green

[Bobbie Breden]

Life as a Mountain

*"Be like a mountain, aim to touch the sky but stay rooted to the
ground" - Anonymous*

I was born as the mountains, thrust into being
Orogeny amid upheaval, conceived of earth, water, air, and fire

I rose up tall and proud, a pinnacle, an apex, a summit
Replete with steep slopes, jagged ridges, sharp peaks,

The winds of change buffeted my surface, created crevices,
Turned my sharp peaks and jagged ridges to rubble

The torrents of life cascaded over my surfaces like a cataract
Wearing my rough face, smoothing and rounding my slopes

Life and change eroded away much of what I had been,
Plundering great chunks, pilfering small nuggets

Yes I had been transformed by nature and circumstance
And the change was accepted without question or regret

My time and season have gone; still I am content
I have existed in harmony with nature and life
Knowing that the only relentless, unremitting constant is change

Orogeny = The process by which the earth's crust is folded and deformed by lateral compression to form a mountain range.

Retired Lady Leatherneck (US Marine), Renaissance woman, and a lover of life's mysteries. I'm interested in how others view the universe, and welcome opportunities to see it through their eyes. Allpoetry.com/Captain_B2

[Amanda Khoury]

Jolt Restrict Vex

Callous fingertips drift up my curves

Caressing gingerly, spanking any unpleasant wayward thoughts

Skepticism mislaid into amnesia fog

Entrusting blissfully

Pledges sworn with a solo hook of pinkies blindly convincing me

that currently is nonidentical to our past

Grip. Clutch. Grasp. Clog.

Seizing my jugular assertively

Vigorously bulldozing any air flow from lungs to nose or nose to

lungs.

Binds of self-condemnation lash onto my wits,

Gone astray are the words of honor that mollified my frazzled

nerves

Withering away as tenderhearted flowers in mid-December

That have been fed velvet poisonous fabrications

With a side of savage repugnance

Paired with deceitful attachment and fraudulent idolization.

Palm sparsely tapping,

Unshackle the blockage with intimate worship: "I have always

imagined you walking down the aisle to meet me"

Repetition inquiry: "why didn't you tap out?"

Unwind my resistance by domineeringly

Aggressive strokes and painful nuzzles.

Repressing protest and disapproval for I am too timid to oppose.

Optimistic pipe dreams sprinkle into my mind; clearing my

fretfulness as simply as powdered sugar can mask the texture of

arsenic.

Amanda Khoury is an avid reader and loves to stay up late to work on her writing while everything is quiet. She enjoys spending time with her family, close friends, playful dogs, and baby cats. Allpoetry.com/Amanda_Khoury

[Te-Wei Peng]

Drinking the Milky Way

Some say rain is the teardrops of the sky
she sobs like a toddler when
her cotton nappy is wet
weeps like a girl when
dark clouds take her blue dress away
and howls like a woman when
the sun deserts her for a finer affair

rain of teardrops
dribbles into rivulets
waterfalls into seas

my face is also a sky
it wails just like normal human beings
yet my grief is like the Titanic
it doesn't float on a creek, a pond or a sea
instead it defies gravity
and soars

into darkness
saline droplets shine as stars
they whirl together into a Milky Way
and blink
and blink
and blink
back the scorching sadness

into a bottle of sparkling
fermenting grief
its taste only we know

Dawnsome is a Taiwnese Australian who lives in Sydney as a
science and religious worker. Poetry is one of her ways to explore
the aesthetic field and connect the world with the beauty of
words. Allpoetry.com/Dawnsome

[Arlice W. Davenport]

Stillness

A great sky
opens within you,
speaks the rarefied
word of affection,
moves from this world
to the next, thrown down
like thunder, tuned up
like the tenor of dreams,
passing through
absence, presence,
askesis, apatheia,
the vast uplift
of the desert,
the inundation
of the sea.

Light crests the cusp
of crumbled rocks.
Tranquility blinds
the inner eye.
It is a matter
of longing,
this arid oasis,
this darkened cave.
You will climb
the barren tree

in stillness,
pluck harmony
from its branches,
hesitate,
meditate,
then repudiate
the Earth.

———————————

I have long been fascinated by mysticism. Its sense of union with
the Ultimate fits perfectly with metaphor: 'This is that.' Thus, this
poem aims to express the heart of one type of mystical practice.
Allpoetry.com/arliced

[Michael Huff]

Violent Cry From A Mockingbird

Every night the song plays again
When I walk outside
The color of red fills the sidewalk
No matter how many streets crossed
A new song is played
This one has a custom rhythm
Close to a drummer's snare
When sitting you see the flash of blue and red
As if a party is near
Walking back home
People shout to keep the party going
When inside quiet noise echo
Morning comes everything is peaceful
I move to a new location
But no matter where I go
The same song plays again as if in my head
Quiet neighborhoods
I hear the birds chirp
Then realized the songs they sing.

_____

Living on edge "With anonymous foes, Be the powerful spirit,
We are Mistello!" I love to write anything that makes you fall in a
story to share and challenge your imagination!
Allpoetry.com/Mistello

[Tina Thrower]

Call of Nature

The sun shines quietly and brightly over a glistening waterfall at
the break of the day
You can see little goldfish swimming with all kinds of pebbles
Deer creep up to get fresh water and rest in the sunshine
you also see squirrels jumping on tree branches nearby
also hear birds chirping loud among the forest.

———————————

My World: I'm a mother and grandma, I love the great outdoors,
bowling, watching movies and going on walks. I'm mainly just
trying to live one day at a time. Allpoetry.com/Icygreenleopard4

[Carole Thewsey]

The Garden Ghost

On restless feet she wanders
through the garden of her life
tall trees of indiscretions past
deline bruised path of strife

Her form oft lingers briefly
near the primulas of grace
before she pirouettes away
in lovers ghost embrace

Chrysanthemums scowl fiercely
at fidelity abstained
and faithful Gladioli bend
their heads in sorrows shame

The passing of her pallid form
brings aconite to bloom
then Angels Trumpet wildly calls
of danger, risk and doom.

The lily's heady perfume speaks
of beauty just skin deep
whilst thoughtless Mandevilla
vines send tendrils meant to trip

Over thyme her flaws revealed
but lesson never learned
So to traverse this acre green
Everlasting must return.

Married, empty nester English nurse who likes to unwind by putting pen to paper, occasionally with success.
Allpoetry.com/Cassie_Hughes

[Marjorie Buyco]

Remembrance

There is a burst of familiarity
an engraved romance
as if your paths have crossed
maybe by the bay
where lovers witness
the sky burn orange,
burn as bright as fireworks -
then subdued by
a subtle zephyr, that knowing
feeling she has settled onto your soul

Warm August weather
and your nervous hands
cold   as glaciers skillfully cupped
her face, trusting   to lift the chin -
a gentle catapult.

Gardenias were quick to blossom
petals eager to fall
like the descent of
a snowflake
on her lips

that first kiss -
soft as a curling foam

of the ocean
surrendering to her waves.

Marjorie is from Illinois. She enjoys writing short stories and
poems, and is in the healthcare business. Writing helps her to
express and share her thoughts and experiences.
Allpoetry.com/Goldistring

[Rick Warrior]

Suite Bugger All

Planet Earth grows empty, our little friends no more...

Butt-air Fly

Encroachment

Bee gone

Centipede all-in

Be lax spider

Vac-ant-see

Moth eaten

Crick-et

Silver fished

De-wormed

Beat all

Term-ite

Earth

Rick was born in New Brunswick, Canada, the middle child of five. He held a variety of interesting jobs in the private and public sector. Allpoetry.com/RickthePoetWarrior

[Arlice W. Davenport]

I Sing the Body Eclectic

1.

I sing the body eclectic.
Its masses of men diversify me,
as I diversify them.
The carpenter, the journeyman,
the farrier, the clerk expand
my world, replenish my soul,
as I expand and replenish theirs.

Who does the yeoman's work
of the self? The soul that shares its part
with the body, perfect in man,
perfect in woman, form of forms?
I say, the soul *is* the body and rises with it.
Each freckle, each wrinkle,
each graying hair lives on, eternal.

2.

I sing the body reflective.
Philosophers enlighten me with ideas,
as I enlighten them with mine.
Who grasps the wonders of the world?
Is it I, myself, or the brain that sees
miraculously with its clear-lensed eyes
and gathers the scenes inwardly like a harvest?

Alone in my far distance, I greet the ancient living ghosts:
Plato and the metaphysicians. Homer and the poets.
Sophocles and the playwrights. Phidias and the sculptors.
Echion and the painters. Thales and the scientists.
Pythagoras and the school of harmony. Euclid and his crazed
geometers. All welcome me as theirs. They are my own.

In the marketplace of opinions, beliefs flow
like wine. I inhale them and they fill my being.
My chest swells with them, my legs yearn
to run with them. They, too, are my own. The criminal,
the marshal, the senator, the apothecary, the mother,
the dock worker, the rail engineer, the prostitute,
the miller, the hunter -- all our mine, their principles
and arguments, their yearnings and hopes.
All are mine, for I contain multitudes.

3.
I sing the body selective.
He who freely chooses liberates me,
as I freely choose and liberate him.
The will is born free, made of impulse
and instinct, grabbing the sweet fruits
of nature as its common store. Woman
chooses man, and man chooses woman.
Together, they inherit the Earth as a plump purse of gold.

I pocket the gold with gusto. It is the wealth
of mankind to expand and progress, to learn
and levitate, far above the warring woes of a world

where tribe murders tribe, where peace eludes
as a deer in a dark wood. We can only give chase.
We can never catch up, not to kill, but to admire
its vast, irreducible majesty, the magnanimity of the cosmos.

Joy is our true nature, laughter our chief expression.
To choose life is the art of being human, it is the American way,
as grandiose as our vast nation, as humble as a newborn babe.
We choose, each in our own way: many faces, but only one,
shared world. We make it one another's. We make it our own.

There likely would be no American poetry without Walt
Whitman. His expansive verse, celebrating the self, the body and
the nation, formed the soaring democratic essence of our legacy as
a country. Allpoetry.com/arliced

[Hunter Aydelott]
Times Line

smiling on time lines
moments caught unaware
driving sunsets open wide
on a chuckled grin stare

photos grand entries flash
elaborate settings cast color
under heat lightning skies
times priceless gifts past

chance meetings reverie
dreams dates first kiss
laughter in many settings
striving for immortalities fate

music solid statues
transcends gold's embrace
upon the guilded stages
dance into memory's gate

I live in Cypress Texas. I'm a rescue diver that loves underwater photography. I also play keyboard in my friend's garage band and have amassed a large music collection. Another hobby is mosaics. Allpoetry.com/Burnside

[Seven Nielsen]

old man ocean

the first time i touched the ocean
my bare feet dug into stubborn sand
heavy/wet /colder than anticipated
less friendly
as the cruel and uneven rhythms
of salty water lapped at me-
the tasting licks
of a heartless old man
the ocean

i suddenly realized
he held the entire earth in one enormous hand
with many names-
he held the souls of many creatures living
but also
he held the remains of many creatures dead
those who had shared
those who had dared
those who had died
beneath his ravenous churn

that summer day
the splashing bubbles and foam at my feet
said, *join me, sojourner-*
i am but a harmless fringe of play-
see how gentle?

you needn't know how to swim-
see how i advance and retreat
leaving your feet safe upon the pearly sand?
see
see how innocent
see?'
he lied

two bones witnessed in the wet-
two bones bleached and dead-
i knew his appetite, this giant old man-
he enticed
he assured
he lied
and then
he devoured
swallowing whole

his many victims were dragged down
by his hidden riptides
heavily drown
all the way down
then
sometimes
just for fun
he vomited their remains
upon his many beaten shores
to mock passers-by
as he lied

Seven is a resident of Provo, Utah and is a television, film, and stage production designer. His hobbies are; poetry, oil painting, and his family which includes 13 wonderful grandchildren. Allpoetry.com/Seven_Nielsen

[Alwyn Barddylbach]

Queen of Spades

Vive la République!

From Meddylgar to Queen of Hearts,
I bid you not about the stolen tarts
nor a cunning knave who craved them.
The koan of this conundrum,
the looking glass had broken.
Who shall be safe in the unwoken
shadow of this dream,
who shall be the Queen?

Roses in the garden,
shall they be black or red?
The Queen of Hearts had been deposed,
unruly passion indisposed,
'the Queen is dead!'
The looking glass had spoken.

Roses in the garden,
shall they be black and white?
The Queen of Spades, her darling maids
and courtiers were marching down the forest glades,
invasion of the night,
the looking glass had woken.

Roses in the garden,
shall they be black or green?
The snow was melting in the palace
and no one here seen Alice,
'long live the Queen!'
said they whom she would pardon.

Roses in the garden,
marigold, peach and yellow.
Basking in the royal sunshine,
humming to a bustling bloodline,
bees and sparrows
to the mission chosen.

A rose on every season,
orchid, thistle and fawn.
From dawn to dusk the thousands gather,
spades and shaman, sister, brother,
how the mighty yawn,
the Queen is in the garden.

Roses in the garden,
snow white on sapphire blue.
Beauty in a moment splendid,
love's devotion never ended,
crisp the morning dew
on a long white clouded mountain.

Roses in the garden,
silver threads in ghostly grey.

One hundred years or more were cast,
a dreadful curse upon the past,
no light of day,
the looking glass had frozen.

From Meddylgar to Queen of Spades,
I bid you not about a rose that fades,
whatever happened to the kingdom,
your darling maids and palace garden?
The looking glass had broken.
Who shall be safe in the unwoken
shadow of this dream,
who *now* shall be the Queen?

'No roses ever in
a garden fair, no rose
a colour spare, no head
a queen or king shall bear'
said Alice,
'a republic can't repair'.

————————————

Prologue, fantasy and nursery rhyme - Roses in the garden, 'they
said she was the garden queen'. One kingdom, birth of the
republic, now the looking glass is broken; in 'Tales from Anyone
Seen Alice' Allpoetry.com/Barddylbach

[Eqra Farrukh]
A beautiful defeat

Eyes were wet, heart became thirsty,
It was a war in which I wanted victory,
Armoured like a knight, brave as a soldier
I was yet assassinated with his words bolder
The ground was dusty, and the war began
I fought to conquer the leader of the clan
He was stronger, therefore I couldn't win
Notwithstanding, I was stronger in skin
Losing the war, I kept my sane to mystery
Incognito and anonymous I made history
The sword that ripped my heart out asunder
Hands that held it like a territory plundered
Summoning close to the war with dying spirit
He the opponent incapacitated me satiric
I kept fighting and fighting back and forth
His eyes gave me a look that no one doth
A queen and king in the battle outright
Queen lost but she was a beautiful dynamite

———————————————

Eqra Farrukh is a current graduate student at the State University of New York, University at Albany. Her genre is versatile and she is a leisure-time writer. Allpoetry.com/Eqra_Farrukh

[Amanda Khoury]

Jarring Regretful Valedictory

Brick by brick
Stone to stone
Bulldoze the confinement that you caused by corrupting my
kindliness and goodwill to forget maliciously criticizing novel
messages
Ricocheting my self-assurance into addiction craving spiteful,
counterfeit endorsement that quickly exploded into maneuvered
manipulation until my whimsical realm had been replaced:
Sorrowful,
Smashed ruins.

Cube by cube
Bond to bond
Under no circumstances were you genuinely generous.
Pestering my devotion to be a chaste women,
Saccharine cock and bull declarations slip into my organs
Erupting like a catapult through my divisions.
Articulating apprehension
Met with
carnal coercion.

Plaque by plaque
Fuse to fuse
Postpone provocative partnership
My barriers have been lacerated severely by stabs of your fingers
Through ruthless ear-piercing perjury

Squalling and bawling for benevolence
Hands together petitioning for toughness within my spirit
Cross-legged with bulldozed gravel piercing my vandalized layers,
Delicately tossing kernels aside for they are to be superseded by tablets.

Boulder by boulder
Slab to slab
Chafe cement between each unpliable and hard as iron gravestone,
Gloominess rubs better against my fragile barrier than relentless tetchiness.
My ejaculated eyes blur chiseling letters that reject a sadistic, cold-blooded, yet still loved narcissist
Not for a moment will these reinvigorated stiffened, unmalleable walls be penetrated by a berserk little boy throwing a wobblier.

Amanda Khoury is an avid reader and loves to stay up late to work on her writing while everything is quiet. She enjoys spending time with her family, close friends, playful dogs, and baby cats. Allpoetry.com/Amanda_Khoury

[Alwyn Barddylbach]

Serpent's Breath

But all this is not about God,
not about nature, not even about woman.
He who says God's wrath for our wrongdoing,
she who says nature versus man
that none shall break the human spirit.
Ours to whale, mine and plunder or not to,
they speak with serpent's breath.

We are not fallen but forever falling and flying,
soaring the empty cosmos
between cataclysmic clouds
that give violent birth and death
to any who draw near.
Eden is a chalice of beauty and poison,
nature's cruel and golden orchard
spinning in the light.

This is not about the human spirit,
nature versus nurture,
for her spirit is the will to survive
against catastrophic odds.
Consider the beasts of the ocean,
the flower in a desert storm,
a tree without a sky,
our many orphaned habitats,

a child without its mother,
we bear her will, her blood!

We are here because we live, we are,
we draw breath from the same ocean,
the same oceans that fly across the galaxy
spinning in the darkness,
protected from apocalypse by
the one mother of all mothers,
she who bears these slings and stones
of fortune in the unbearable emptiness.

But this is not about her nor us,
the earthquake nor the storm, God's speed.
This is our joy and tragedy, life and death, our lot!
The Universe asks not who's to blame
only our foolish arrogance, our indifference
and they who in ignorance and anger claim,
they speak with serpent's breath.

Revelation 8.1 'And when he had opened the seventh seal, there
was silence in heaven...' Conscious Universe: 'He' who breathes
first in the Garden of Eden - (Emrys) Blue Mountains
Allpoetry.com/Barddylbach

[Andy Sprouse]

Still on Patrol

Can you hear the whispers
brought on by the wind storming?
Carried true by the harpers,
the tale the howls are forming?

Came a knock at the farmer's door,
a mailed fist with a fate to turn.
A sob, a wail, a call to war,
a boy, a son, home soon to yearn.

Soon a soldier strode from youth,
to the beat of the king's drum.
A shield his hide, a sword his tooth,
his pack stood the night to come.

Oh for the heroes of men,
the ones who hold the line -
oh for the kin behind,
the ones who hold to hope.

Silence broke to a thunderous horn,
the battle joined with the savage horde.
On a bloody tide he thus was borne,
death he granted and fury he roared.

Silence returned with a blade's sigh,
sanguine as it was ripped away.
A keen, a dirge, a mother's cry,
a man, a son, home soon to lay.

Oh for the heroes of men,
the ones who hold the line -
oh for the kin behind,
the ones who hold to hope.

A place to rest he was given,
a peace he has not taken.
To guard, to serve he is driven,
his will, his resolve unshaken.

So when you see a warrior's mound,
shed not a tear to hear the bugle -
hark rather the marching sound,
for he yet walks the vigil.

———————————

Andy Sprouse is a young musician, writer and woodworker. Like
many, poetry is his way of thinking out loud, of sharing his
experiences. Allpoetry.com/wolfdrummer13

[Tina Thrower]

Forever

What is alwayz n forever:
day, week, month, year or a lifetime?
To me would be Ronald Jones Sr. or like the farmers song or
restaurant or the man of the hour so to speak.
Could be sweetie pie or Miles Similey, like a similey line at work
or miles and miles you travel on the roads.
either way Chariots of Fire like the movie .
In the sky above or ground below; both men are Heaven to me.

———————————

My World: I'm a mother and grandma, I love the great outdoors,
bowling, watching movies and going on walks. I'm mainly just
trying to live one day at a time. Allpoetry.com/Icygreenleopard4

[Judith Meade]

Sweet Magnolia

O' how I love the months February through June, I walk the brick
path of Louisiana
Jazz music flows out into the streets and the sweetness of
magnolia is in the air
The magnolia flower has many scent's the citrus honey to the
sweet tart of the bloom.
I stroll through the streets and think how the meaning, magnolia
is beauty, sweet, and love and how it makes my day brighter,
softer, full of warmth.
Jazz music fits right in place as I wander on and enjoy my paradise
as long
Till the flowers dies and jazz doors shut
I will wait with patience till I hear the music and then I know you
are ready to bloom open again , paradise I will roam once again

---

I am a grandmother who is raising 3 grandkids. I enjoy reading
and I am learning to paint. I enjoy poetry and I am a person who
hide things inside so writing is how I get the feelings out.
Allpoetry.com/Judithmeade

[Shelly Nichols]

Rain

Take a bath in the rain..
he'll wash your shadows away..
wash over my skin.
follow the wind..
for the man..
who's heart... smells like the rain.

California is my home..
But my heart breathes easily in Arizona.
I write from my dreams..
I write about people I dearly love..
I write to keep my heart peaceful..
I write to entertain poetic genius.

Allpoetry.com/Shelly_Nichols

[Judith Meade]

Sweet Magnolia

O' how I love the months February through June, I walk the brick
path of Louisiana
Jazz music flows out into the streets and the sweetness of
magnolia is in the air
The magnolia flower has many scent's the citrus honey to the
sweet tart of the bloom.
I stroll through the streets and think how the meaning, magnolia
is beauty, sweet, and love and how it makes my day brighter,
softer, full of warmth.
Jazz music fits right in place as I wander on and enjoy my paradise
as long
Till the flowers dies and jazz doors shut
I will wait with patience till I hear the music and then I know you
are ready to bloom open again , paradise I will roam once again

———————————

I am a grandmother who is raising 3 grandkids. I enjoy reading
and I am learning to paint. I enjoy poetry and I am a person who
hide things inside so writing is how I get the feelings out.
Allpoetry.com/Judithmeade

[Alma Ray]

Our Colored Landscape

Blue, yellow and amber cover the
horizon,
Fluffy, pure white clouds float along on a
silvery background, the glorious sun rising.

A forest full of staggering green and orange
leaved trees speckled with red,
Animals such as the bobcat, deer, foxes chipmunks too; differing
in personalities, all of purebred.

Insects of different type of beauty flit about
doing their jobs to survive this life of wonder,
Olive, lavender, cobalt, yellow, black, and corals; with wings of
color and some of clarity, they are made up of the entire spectrum,
all meant to go about freely both above ground and under...

Meadows of green grass with wild flowers have colors of citrine,
purple, pinks and red; they offer such feelings of calm and
comfort, peacefully,
Rays of golden sunlight glisten upon all of
God's creation giving off a quiet soothing comfort ceaselessly.

We move about, forgetting to stop and
see, then explore or appreciate all of life's
blessings and grace,
We gaze around us and realize that our world is truly one of

intricate splendor,
it cannot be replaced.

Beautifully painted skies, fields of lovely
flowers, prismatic colored insects, multi
dimensional animals and magnificent lands
for you to witness, taking shape,
Just open your eyes, my fellow brothers and
sisters, help me embrace the gift of our multi faceted world and
add a vivid, magnificence to each of our own existence, let us
enjoy the elegance of all that is availed to us in our colored
landscape.

———————————

A poet is who I am, heart, mind, and soul. I write from the
depths of my being, whatever it may be that flows.
I'm also a mother and a wife who dearly loves her family and
writing. Allpoetry.com/ARay

[Carmen Melton Bennett]

Confetti Confessions

Chardonnay stains on worn carpet
A broken glass or two
A few burnt meatballs in the crockpot
A pile of half-deflated balloons

An abandoned bowl of Rotel dip
A forgotten set of keys
A few bubbles dance in a bottle
Melted candles drip impatiently

A tiara and banner for the Queen-
"Happy 21!", oh, what an epic day
Selfies with friends; a kiss from a "maybe"
Pictures posted, tag away

Miss Kitty is hiding in the bedroom
Unsure of the night's events
Apartment 212 smells peculiar
A blend of adulthood and innocence

Tomorrow will bring the sunlight
The Hoover and maybe regret
But for tonight the music lingers
Like confetti swirling in her head

A songwriter and publisher in South Alabama with over 400 songs to her credit, Carmen recently dipped the pen in the poetry well for the first time in decades. A new outlet has been unleashed! Allpoetry.com/Carmen_Melton_Bennett

[Patricia Marie Batteate]

Donations for Sale

You peaceful people
Going about your lives
Treated like sheep
Under the knife

A commodity to slaughter
Raped and enslaved
Marked as a donor
Erecting no grave

Tissue type and blood
The first rule of business
Your organs to harvest
From those of the fittest

They come unexpected
The call came through
A perfect match
For money to accrue

They tie you down
Awake and aware
They cut out your heart
With neither a care

Thrown into a furnace
No name to remember
Unused body parts
Savagely dismembered

Pray for these people
Please don't ignore
We know this is wrong
We've been here before.

_____

I am a 7th generation Californian. I am an engineer, poet and
artist. I could see poets inheriting the earth.

Allpoetry.com/Patricia_Marie

[Sindy Mitchell]

Empty Promises

The brisk wind smites icy windowsills,
Broken heart, broken dreams,
The cracked door shudders and bangs,
Silence begins.

Blow wind blow,
As trees lower their heads,
Your protection was influenced by false lips,
Hurting my heart.

Flattering, smooth-tongued utterances,
Upon an ample figure,
A red-haired coiffeur,
With a bulging black suit.

He walks away,
In a thumping stomp,
His somber shadow vanishes,
Memories flash out of existence.

Drops dribbling down pale cheeks,
The moon overcasts the night sky,
Your lips were enmeshed with elegant words,
Leaving me with your empty promises.

Sindy Mitchell is a teacher and writer with a master's degree in Guidance and Counseling. She studies law, opera, electric piano and classical piano. She lives in Toronto, Canada.
Allpoetry.com/S._Mitchell

[Hunter Aydelott]
Ticking Time

money's doubts seem rebuffed
handshakes to fist blaze together
shaping societies willingness
glowing wishes granted
on phoenixes wing wishing

blind timelines loving embrace
clocks tightrope spinning wishes
fight nightmares clock unwinding
revisited spin of lost memory
in logjams past wishes death grip

when is always forever now?
free your mind of ticking time

I live in Cypress Texas. I'm a rescue diver that loves underwater
photography. I also play keyboard in my friends garage band and
have amassed a large music collection. Another hobby is mosaics.
Allpoetry.com/Burnside

[Joel Ortiz-Rosas]

Your Flower

I was your flower, bound to your garden,
with a stem of deep green and petals of blue.
not to be touched or let my scent linger
around anyone if they were not you.

You left me alone, you left me unguarded
and a passerby fell in love with my hue.
He charmed me with words, offered me
a world that seemed too good to be true.

He plucked me from the ground
and left a hole where I was at there.
You mourned and moved on as my
fragrance eventually dissolved in the air.

Now that I'm here chained to his yard,
I have been forced to put aside my pride.
Admit that I've learned that the grass
isn't always greener on the other side.

_____

I am Puerto Rican born in New Jersey. Poetry gave me a voice
when I felt I couldn't really express how I was feeling, Thru it I
found myself and God. Allpoetry.com/Jupiter_Joel

[Andy Sprouse]

Behind the Sole

Days ago, in the realm of sleep
I stepped into another man's shoes.
When I walked out of them,
from the dream I woke weeping.

These shoes were on the feet
of a black youth of sixteen years.
I saw through his eyes,
and Jim Crow still ruled the day.

I saw color through his eyes,
not the black and white of the screens.
I saw a restaurant filled with laughter,
a family of smiles and of love.

I saw a boy with not much schooling,
trying to learn how to write a sign.
I saw the mood shift through his eyes,
when brutes walked in with hate in theirs.

I saw, through his eyes now tearing,
black and white - yelling and screaming.
I saw the struggle to keep writing,
as slurs fell like the blows that followed.

I saw not what his hands were weaving,
while focused on pale beasts posing as men.
Not 'til he shakingly held up his work,
and I saw his eyes land on his words.

"Those men won't let me speak,
because my words might heal."

I stepped into another man's shoes
days ago, in the realm of sleep.
I know not the cobbler, nor the sender,
but from the message I woke weeping.

Andy Sprouse is a young musician, writer and woodworker. Like
many, poetry is his way of thinking out loud, of sharing his
experiences. Allpoetry.com/wolfdrummer13

[S. Libellule]

Magnetic North

"Death is the magnetic north of poetry" ~ Billy Collins

No need for navigational charts
some poetic sextant on the starboard side
since the truth can no longer hide
for death is vitally this
(without all of the usual fuss)
poetry's magnetic north

Helping us lay a course
letting us return again
to a life where purpose does remain
although we keep the end of days
in the old familiar ways

Denial
avoidance
contrivance
perhaps a self medicating vice

While it is only within the poem
we truly arrive back home
at ease within our expiring skin

As the needle again points north
towards death and finding life's worth

From Alabama, Libellule enjoys reading and writing poetry.
Strongly influenced by Mary Oliver and Billy Collins, Libellule's
poetry is introspective with a reverence for language and the
everyday. Allpoetry.com/LilDragonFly

[Elizabeth Zumbahlen-Ruperez]
Spools of Thread

Life the weaving threads, colorful spools of thread
never to dread from that dreadful look on your face.

My heart sings a love song, for the one and only love
that calls me home, dear home sweet home.

My feet like floating leaves skimming afloat
on the unbroken mirror, only to break when the air's not cold.

Hands wave in the distance reflecting no distance
between the lives we have, to the lives we had to let go.

Colorful spools spin unwrapping each color
alas to tightly twill and wrap around my soul.

Begging to free this contained spirit
my tied down dying spirit, prays to freely roam.

Roaming amidst the spirals of colorful threads with no dreads
millions streaming and weaving heavenly rainbow paintings in my
head.

_____

Teacher, storyteller and writer born in Illinois (USA) living in
Spain and currently part of the Cantabrian Public School's
bilingual program. Allpoetry.com/Poemartgallery

[Willie Flud]

Paradise in blue

Paradise in blue
A quiet walk along the
Shore, no one else just
Me and you.

Your blue sweater pulled
Up right, because the wind
Crept up and gave you
A fright

But I was there to
Keep you safe as we
Went in search of the
Perfect place

For a front seat
In paradise!

I am a retired OEF Vet, from Queens NY, who enjoys the spoken
word and sharing it with those like myself. I hope you like it,
cause it comes from the heart! Allpoetry.com/Blacque

[Wanda Thibodeaux]

I Am a Writer

Self doubt?
I am riddled with it.
I suffer from metaphor mania.
I seek the cure for the common poem.
I scream similes.
It is the tears of the dogwood,
the wind's hymn,
the color of blue-grass,
and love...
sturdy as mountain laurel
that I have learned from.
I am a writer.

Dreams, dry, like leaves
on curled, crispy feet
are wind-swept into that dark abyss
where the past hides.
I write lyrics to warm the bareness.
I am the snow-steeped hills
before the sun.
I am the reflection of forever
in the depths of moss-bound creek beds.
I am sheet music for the river's song.
I am a writer.

In this forest of man,
I am the narrative told by tall sycamores,
the artistry of magnolia blossoms,
I am the flag for freedom.
My smoking gun...
The power of an outstretched hand.
I am my brother's keeper.
Southern skies enwrap me.
I am synchronized with the stars.
These lines are my legacy.
I weep words.
I am a writer.

_____

I was born in Tennessee and lived mesmerized by the gorgeous trees growing there. Louisiana matched that green beauty and now I am in the West (By God) VA mountains. God's nature is magnificent! Allpoetry.com/LouisianaLady

[Joanne Zylstra]

Secluded

The quietness is unbearable,
Draws you in to a world of deafness,
The trees devise words, by the rustling of branches,
The wind whispers, but utters no speech,
Secluded in this world.

People yearn for this solitude,
Removed from the hustle and bustle of city life,
A place with incredible charm,
The quiet sounds of nature.

Both beautiful and terrifying,
As the sunset fade from tranquil orange to blackness
eerie sounds interrupt the calm,
The howling of coyotes embraces your body
the scream from the peak of a tree
all this adds to the cacophony of nighttime sounds.

A feeling of being lost in the captivating place
Forsaken by humans and embraced by sounds
I have felt this feeling of maladapted to my surroundings.

Married since 1984 to my husband, Tom and we have two
children, Andrew and Allison that amaze us every day.
Allpoetry.com/Mommy_Bear

[Ken Makepeace]

A Country Lane

Walking through a country lane
Scattered trees surrounded by
daffodils, so pretty to see
Cows grazing in the field
Spring lambs jumping around
happily as though they didn't have
a care
Hedge rows covered with colour
and beauty, what a sight to see
All this just walking through
a country lane

―――――――――――――

Makepeaceken is from North Wales, in the UK, where I have
lived most of my life. I took up writing after going on course at a
local college when I was in my mid forties
Allpoetry.com/LonePoet

[Kamla Williams]

Freedom Reined

She was five years old when she first went to school
They told her that learning would free her from being a fool
And how lucky she was that her schooling was free
For not everyone had the opportunity
Showers of freedom rained on her so graciously
She was free to be anything she wanted to be
Doctor, lawyer, engineer, or mayor of the city
Counselor, comedian, cook, or captain on the sea

Five days a week, her nose was in a book
Studying hard was what it took
To become the lawyer she wanted to be
As young as she was, injustices were plain to see
The other two days were spent running and jumping, climbing
trees
Singing and playing and shouting in the breeze
No boundaries were set to curb her way
Queen Freedom reigned in her field of play

But at the edge of the playground, a stranger stood
Who looked at her frolicked as long as she could
And one day when she ventured after a straying ball
"Hello pretty girl," she heard him call
He looked like a lion in a book she had read
Eyes lusting on its prey before it was dead

Fear gripped her being and she started to run
His laugh behind her echoing his fun

Her days in the play-ground became less and less
And when the curse overtook her she was in a mess
No sooner she was summoned by her mother and dad
To console her, she thought, they sensed she was sad
But no such comfort was on the agenda that day
Instead, she was told that she was going away
To be married to the stranger who gave her the fright
The lion that glared at its prey with his might

No amount of begging and pleading at their feet
Would change their minds from this wicked deceit
They told her it was a sacrifice she had to make
To make things better for the family's sake
And so she was given to this strange old man
A twelve-year-old girl who once had a plan
Her freedom was reined in like a bucking wild horse
Her will was broken by excessive force

There was no way out, no room to escape
Silently she screamed during rape after rape

Kamla Williams is from Trinidad & Tobago. She is an introvert who expresses herself best in her writing.

Allpoetry.com/Kamla_Williams

[Andrew Lee Joyner]

Acting

In theaters near you
A new movie has come out
About blood and gore

Not meant for children
The true horrors hide nowhere
Watch out for yourself

To play a true murderer
Takes the mind of a killer
"Could you act it out?"

———————————

When I started writing it became a hobby of mine and now it's
my life, I love to read and write. My inspiration is life, my sister is
my muse Allpoetry.com/Twiztid_Pennywise

[Glenn Houston Folkes III]

Our Irish Luck

Looking for a four-leaf clover,
Waiting until the battle is over,
We have been losing our lives because we got drunk,
From Ireland to the States, we packed our trunks,
Irish at birth and until after we are dead,
You can admire us, we are Irish,
That is enough said.

_____

I am a Native Texan. I started writing poetry at Lake Highlands High School and have various forms of expression. In this stage of my career, I have been leaning towards self-expression. Allpoetry.com/Barkdream69

[Iris Salters]

Be promoted by God, Demoted let the devil

be charge

Promoted when repent
Demoted when didn't come in
Promoted when gotten saved
Demoted when didn't come his way
Promoted came to God   Demoted didn't work hard
Promoted living right
Demoted didn't fight

Promoted knew his name
Demoted were a shame
Promoted coming church
Demoted got hurt
Promoted being obedient
Demoted let them
In
Promoted trusted in God Demoted failed apart
Promoted helping someone
Demoted didn't get it done
Promoted heart were good
Demoted didn't do what should
Promoted didn't give up
Demoted didn't know your stuff
Promoted pass the test

Demoted when didn't give your best
Promoted still here
Demoted didn't give
Promoted didn't let go
Demoted didn't know
Promoted ask for giving
Demoted didn't listening
Promoted came in
Demoted for your sins
Promoted being a blessing
Demoted when didn't do the lesson

Hello My name is Iris Salters were born in Greenville South
Carolina most of my life spend in Washington DC became
resident of Prince George County Maryland
Attend Greater Morning Star.

Allpoetry.com/Lil_Lady

[Andrew Lee Joyner]

The destiny path

Dancing of the soul, emotions felt, voices say right and wrong,
I'm neutral
Lost in limbo,
Between life and death

Self reflect to find the best version of yourself to convey;
your past turmoil is the key
you must look deep within yourself,
Discover your true self
Sort out your inner demons to win,
Only then, will you find peace over sin

With time comes wisdom,
Carry on, to find freedom
Follow a path of your own making,
Together, apart
Universal

When I started writing when I was young and it has become a
hobby of mine, My sister is my muse, inspiration comes from
imagination. Allpoetry.com/Twiztid_Pennywise

[Judith L Harmon]

May you never be as fucked up as me

May you never be as fucked up as me, May your life be trouble-free

May people be honest with you, May you always remain true.

Don't let your guard down for a minute....for a minute is all that they need.

To use you and to abuse you, and all in the name of greed....

May you always be you...Innocent and blame-free, And thank the Gods that you can never be me.

Judith was Born in Seattle in 1965, Married & divorced now enjoying being a new grandma to Jack Zeus (2020) (Mother to Shianne, Jack's mom) Son Dakota and two angels. (Shawnee 1996 & Brandon 2012) Allpoetry.com/Judith_Harmon

[Lorri Ventura]

Mom

Born on St. Joseph's feast day
She hoped to merit his protection
And she lived,
Until she didn't.
Her spirit drifted away
Writhing
In the smoke
Of the cigarettes
She puffed obsessively

Lorri Ventura is a retired special education administrator living in Massachusetts. Her poems have appeared in several anthologies. Allpoetry.com/Lorri_Ventura

[Sean Cooke]

[For Billy the Staffordshire Bull Terrier]

It was on January 3rd your padded feet took a walk at four pm or just after. As you sniffed the green grass and felt the cold chill you knew you were coming to the end of your final chapter.

You no longer ran, and your four legs took it slow our emotions battled with each other and the hardest decisions come from within, to let you keep suffering even the devil would call that a sin.

At thirteen you passed away that is an unlucky number some say, but you gave us a life full of pleasure and joy wandering through bushes and leaves, your eyes and nose on radar looking for your bone and toy.

Stroking your red and white hair and seeing your eyes fill with delight, I will confess I shed a tear writing this but I know the time is just right.

Rest in peace Billy my four legged friend my memories of you mean it never comes to an end.

———————————

I am a 31 year old man from northern England, reading and writing poetry is now a satisfying and productive part of my life. I thank my mother and father deeply and all those who read my poetry. Allpoetry.com/Arsenalfan30

I'm Emotionally Bankrupt

I've taken all
I can take
Given all I
can give
I feel like
someone
disconnected,
Surrounded by
people so inept
Just

Emotionally Bankrupt

Some people
Are so corrupt
So
Inept
All they do is
disrupt, disconnect
Others lives
by telling
Lies,
creating chaos
And dispise you
For no apparent

Reason. I call
these People

Emotionally Bankrupt

They have no love
For self or others
When they speak
It's obvious
they seek
To steal, kill
and destroy
Nothing good ever
Comes out of their
Mouth
they
Appear to exist
To make others feel
Bad, by finding fault
In all they see
I believe they are
The epitome of
misery
No feelings at all
Just

Emotionally Bankrupt

Socially inept
Seeking to disrupt

Everything and
Everybody
What a lonely person
A lonely place
To be
They must be
Unhappy
Just

Emotionally Bankrupt

Catherine Sales former Ed Counselor from Compton CA.
Catherine holds several Master's Degree in Psychology, Education,
Human Behavior & Education Adm Cred. Former President
PA4C M.H .Advocacy 501C. Allpoetry.com/Cathysalesmftpoet

[Emeli Dion]

Whispers of Love

Our love could not be shown.
We were forced to hide it.
But the woodland creatures knew;
The plants could discern it.

Love whispered to me,
Through the leaves in the garden.
It could not be seen,
But I could feel its presence.

It was in the flowers.
It shone down in the moonlight.
The birds whistled its tune,
While crickets made a harmony.

Though love cannot always be in view,
We know it still exists.
We may not completely understand it,
But we do know that it is needed.

––––––––––––––––––

Emeli Dion lives in a small town located in New Hampshire.
When she isn't studying for school or working, she enjoys writing,
painting, crocheting, and playing guitar.
Allpoetry.com/Emeli_Dion

[April Sache]

Hope for a better tomorrow

Every day is new
cherish them through and through
hold your head up high
look to the clouds and the sky

show appreciation for life
share positive notions
hope for a better tomorrow

if you believe
pray positive prayers
to receive better outcomes for your days

wish the bad away
don't play the devil's advocate
for each day is new
and you can be too

Hope for a better tomorrow
for yourself and for your neighbors
get on the good path
stay on track

speak positive notions
spread positive energy

so that you don't hold yourself back
in any entity

Life is a game
play yours well
stay positive with the way you carry yourself

manage your own life
don't gamble on others

do everyone a favor by
being a good neighbor
manipulate no one

for the introvert
speak and spread positivity

for the extrovert
speak and spread positivity

this will bring a better tomorrow.

_____

I am from Gary, Indiana. I have 6 books on amazon.com 'My
World with a Horse,' ' A single lady's life,' 'Lavender Love,' 'All I
want in a man,' 'Life of the Party' and 'Adventures of Fairyland'
Allpoetry.com/April_Sache

[Lisa F. Raines]

Vantage Point

The man in front of the mirror
The man in the mirror
The man behind the mirror

Who is it we see?
Id, Ego, Superego
What is the vantage point?

The mind of the id
Looks into the mirror, and
Sees the ego
The man he wants to be

But hidden behind that mirror
Is the superego
Who controls what the man sees

How he sees it
Exposes his
Vantage Point

AlisRamie is from North Carolina, USA.
Interests include: philosophy, history, international relations,
poetry, art, design, jazz, funk rock, and some good old soul.
Allpoetry.com/AlisRamie

[Jacob Davis]

Lukewarm Tea

Waiting by the window
Hour after hour, asking if you were near
My life, unlike theirs, will never be crystal clear
Yet you still ponder why we're in this limbo

I love you, but I don't know why
Sometimes at night, I sit and sigh
The tears never seem to dry
When I sit alone and begin to cry

I don't know how to escape this toxic relationship
You will never give me what I truly want: companionship
I ask for money to fill my damaged heart
To me, it makes up for all of those years of being apart

Do you know me?
Really... do you?
Do you know you make me feel like a bother?
Do you know that my biggest fear is being just "a father"?

'Cause that's what you've been to me
A ceremonial title unable to enable a sense a of glee
A haunted house has never scared me
I'm used to feeling the ghost of a person who I cannot see

Sure, you didn't miss all of the milestones

Yet you still talk to me in that phony, facetious tone

Sorry, but those little moments, those profound days when you ignored my plea

Have evaporated like the steam from lukewarm tea

A current sophomore attending the University of Miami, Jacob Davis is currently pursuing a degree in architecture. On his spare time, Davis' hobbies include interior design, photography, and writing. Allpoetry.com/Jaked25

[Cindy Phan]

Parasyte

Your eyes are like thorns that pierce through my soul.
The space for your heart has become a black hole.
Your tongue dipped in venom, it slides down my throat.
Play me over and over, a dangerous note.

Your hands are like spiders that creep on my skin.
Your bed's full of needles, they all have me pinned.
I'll never get back all the peace that you took.
Your scent is a drug, but I'm so fucking hooked.

I choke on my words and don't know where to start,
As the noose gets tighter to rip me apart.
I have every excuse to turn things around,
But this love comes in waves, it leaves me to drown.

I'm so lost and confused, I don't know what's right.
There's no bullets left to load up this fight.
When I try to think it over, the longing impedes.
I just need to cut you out, and let myself bleed.

———————————

Cindy Phan is a dark poet and adventure photographer from
Seattle, WA. You can find her on instagram under the username
@cindyphantastic. Allpoetry.com/cindyphantastic

[Lonna Lewis Blodgett]

Dear Captain

Dear Walt, my precious poet you incite meaning
With words that inspire, your pen's human truth
Every phrase I write, I share your journey to recite
With steadfast care, each thought longstanding
So we can serve our poet's path with broad, robust and vast
Understanding from the knowledge that history leads us
Through each of our possible destinies, for Dear Captain
You pilot our hearts, minds and mortal lives!

You turn each elegy into a flower's song so gloriously told
Exquisite pluck and promises burn the stage you create
Engaging substance so bold, you discorrupt the body
To save our mortal souls to mold us to our redemption
For human quests must pave and unfold the stories
from where your center thrives to share
Emanating towards from our needful dreaming within
As our eyes read your masterpiece tempting to dare
A footpath that bares our spirit to be alive!

Dear beloved Walt, revived in a summer's blade of grass
You know the story well my, friend from our beginnings
And from our past, of cradles endlessly rocking
We grow with barefoot senses to touch the earth
In places where few can go, we are alone and fatal
Yet your faith spreads light over the fences of things we cannot be
To enrapture the enduring plight in our minds to set us free

We find your verity and kindness, our lives assured!

I have spent a lifetime searching for answers regarding truth and meaning. I have found in the art of poetry the uniqueness of its intrinsic language as the conveyance of the human experience. Allpoetry.com/Lonna_Blodgett

[Julie Liverman]

My Love Is So Deep

When you step into my light,
You will feel My energy.

My love is so deep.

When your lips touch mine you will feel electricity.

My love is so deep.

When our bodies touch each other.
You will feel like you're in a fantasy where birds are singing, the
trees are blossoming, the smell of sweet honey from our friendly
Queen Bee .

As we floating around her tree as our body drips sweet sweat all
over the Queen family.

A cloud forms, it starts to rain all over our bodies
Which switch us to another fantasy.

My love is so deep.

As you enter my ocean A wrath of waves splashes against our
bodies, drifting us down deeper into the sea.

The dolphins, sharks,and fishes swim around our bodies, feeling
our vibrations.

My love is so deep.

As you exit my fantasy, you will always remember me.. Julie Luvunoless now you are a part of my energy.

My love is so deep.

I'm Julie Liverman, writing with the name Julie Luvunoless. I enjoy writing erotica short stories and poems, especially on a rainy night while having a glass of wine and zoning out. I thank God for my gift. Allpoetry.com/Julie_Luvunoless

[Alma Ray]

Night of the Were

The skies are black, being kissed by the pale
full moon,
The girl waits in the clearing of the forest
humming a tune.
A crack echoes, an eerie chill comes over the night,
Where is her love, for she is frightened now and wishes she had a
light.

Trees all around her bend, as if to listen closely
to her beating heart,
A crash sounds through the willows, now she
fears she must depart.
As she runs the beaten path back, the one the
lovers know well,
She is confronted by a figure of horrifying size
that freezes her, as if in some spell.

The creature growls, moans and somehow, she
recognizes the tone,
This monster is her beloved in his true form, she sees now, for in
the moonlight his eyes have shown.
She falls to her knees and calls to her love, "come, get me",
He advances, whimpers and without control bites, then lifts her
to carry her away somewhere they can be free.

Morning comes, and they both awaken disheveled yet rested and blissfully unaware,
That tonight when the moon rises again, they will hear the call, feel the pull, and both become a were.

_____

A poet is who I am, heart, mind, and soul. I write from the depths of my being, whatever it may be that flows.
I'm also a mother and a wife. Allpoetry.com/ARay

[Lisa Mailliard]

What Do I Know

Discounted, misunderstood, neglected, hated
Labeled, judged, young men incarcerated
flashing lights, terror, hands on the wheel.
Suspicion, fear, no one cares how you feel
No sudden movements, the "talk" with your sons
Chased down while jogging, accusers, guns
No choices, dealing, expensive cars
Lost in an instant, handcuffs, scars
Struggle, hard work, family ties
Accused, murdered, a mother cries
Tied up and dragged down the country road
The color of his skin no longer showed.
Shot while sleeping, a knee on your neck
Killed while watching TV in your own apartment.
Taking your last breath, begging for your mom
treated like an animal, until you are eternally calm.
A mistake they say, your race didn't matter
No accountability taken, faith and trust shattered
Riots in the streets, frustration boiling over
Screaming, "Black lives matter!" as they took cover.
Our first black president said, "Yes we can!"
But did we? Could we? When will hate end?
Was this finally the moment when the tide would turn?
Would this man change minds, or would more crosses burn?
We had leadership of a different color for 8 short years.

Did we move forward as a nation, with more love and less fear?
He endured endless attacks as his black hair turned gray
While the underbelly of the nation simmered, waiting for their day.
Our hopes were dashed as they emerged from under their rocks.
Pent-up hatred and resentment roared back on middle American blocks.
Put them back in their place, push civil rights back a century
How dare people of color think they're equal and worthy.
What do I know about this systemic bias and hate?
Does the color of my skin permit my anger at their fate?
Is my concern seen as patronizing, looked at with scorn?
What could I know about what they've dealt with, since the day they were born?
What do I know of their century's old fight?
What do I know of intolerance and fright?
Have I ever felt the evil look of suspicion?
Been followed in stores, a conviction, their mission?
Have I ever been passed over for the job because of my name?
The color of my skin gives me privilege and a better shot at fame.
So much I cannot comprehend, but there is one thing I do know
I can teach my children tolerance and to speak up as they grow.
Respect is key and listening is a must
Acknowledgment and empathy are what earn trust.
Be mindful of your responses, and keep an open mind
Be consistent with your friendship, be an advocate, and kind.
Speak up when you see injustice and bigotry
Stand up and stand by those who live with this day to day.
It's your duty to pass these values on to the next generation

Only time can erase outdated ideals and evil intentions.
To those who have been discounted, misunderstood, and hated.
Please know you have allies in us, however belated.

––––––––––––––––––––

Mailliardwrites helps get it. I'm in So. California where I teach, garden, color, and write. I'm new at this and find it extremely therapeutic and rewarding when the words work! Words are Power. Allpoetry.com/Mailliardwrites

[Ms. Angela B. Spragg]
Never Stop Trying

If the battle is so hard,
What about the war?
If everything is a battle,
What is your war?

My battle is won but the war remains,
For this war to be conquered, in truth I must remain,
War is a journey of extreme toxicity,
Why fear now of its proximity?
Remember the joy of victorious battle,
Let's move forward for your biggest rattle.

Draw your strength from your cornerstone,
Why do you feel you are so alone?
Don't let the ego fool you again,
Keep going and going until you are victorious again.

Angela B. Spragg is from England, UK. She is Certified
International Self perspective Coach. Her poems are the about the
conversation with a soul. In the noise we forget the SELF has a
voice. Allpoetry.com/Abspragg

[Alma Ray]

Purple Butterfly

On a beam in a barn sits a small silky, cream colored cocoon,
What lies within will not come out the same as it went in under
this moon.

She was born pretty, no frills, overlooked by even her own family
at times,
All she could hope for is that one day would come for things to
change, and be sublime.

So many around her seem so vivid though not one is purple
curiously, and glorious in their unique nature,
She daydreams of nuances so marvelous it must only be for
royalty or greater.

The day comes for her long sleep , she weaves her silk, tucks in and
readies for the transformation,
Her time is peaceful as several suns and moons pass, during this
period of gestation..

One beautiful golden sunned morning her silk sack opens and she
blinks the sleep from her now brilliant blue eyes and out she
crawls,
She stretches and her wings pop open, and all those around her
are enthralled.

For this simple caterpillar now possesses beauty so stunning,
colors all around so splendid, catching everyone's eye,
She is unique because she carries in her new colored wings, the
color of royalty, she's now known as the purple butterfly.

A poet is who I am, heart, mind, and soul. I write from the
depths of my being, whatever it may be that flows.
I'm also a mother and a wife. Allpoetry.com/ARay

[Steven McDaniel]

Celestials

Ode to my Sun and Moon.

How beautifully above this world your loom.

Spiraled behind clouds and standing in front of the stars.

Here I stand bound by the Earth's bars.

Tough my eyes are dim.

I may gaze at your beauty through a lens.

From dawn's beauty

To sunset's cruelty,

I gaze upon hopeful days and lonely nights.

Guided by your celestial light,

I will do what is right.

Before you I stand,

With my arms outstretched across the land.

I fall forth to embrace you my Mother Earth.

You are not only our cradle but our womb.

For so long you have also been our tomb.

To the stars we are drawn to your beauty above all, Venus.

A home you actually are but will you accept us?

A home to mold and a home to be.

If only from our greed we would flee.

Strange dancer with dancers who do go round,

Sistered in the heavens with the most magnificent rings ever found.

Before you stands the red warrior,

Passed by a lonely voyager.

Journeyed past Jovians of ocean blue.

Your eyes capture for us something new.

Past rock and ice you found a loving sphere.

Out into the cosmos despite our fears,

We sent you out into the cold.

A record of ourselves we mold.

As the cold sets into my bones,

Your beautiful lights sing to my soul in harmonic tones.

As our lights fade and all my hope is gone,

I feel the warmth of the Sun's dawn.

I have always loved writing poetry though when I first started I was never good at it. I worked hard to use it to express my soul when all I had was paper and pen. It became an outlet for my voice. Allpoetry.com/Salem_Macanbhais

[Ken Makepeace]
We Were All Waiting

We were all waiting, and hoping,
but it never happened - it never
occurred, because they were
waiting for you. I was too, but you
never came, never explained.

Where did you go? What did you
do? Someone said you went to
the zoo, but you didn't let me come
too.

Now we are wondering where you are
We are thinking you are going to be
a big movie star and be driven around in
an expensive car.

But remember, when you do become
rich and famous, I knew you first.
We met in a bar and you were
dying of thirst.

Makepeaceken is from North Wales, in the UK, where I have
lived most of my life. I took up writing after going on course at a
local college when I was in my mid forties
Allpoetry.com/LonePoet

[Bobbie Breden]

Whisperings in the Garden

Plop, plick, plock,
It begins to rain
Plip, plop, plock, here and there,
And then suddenly the heavens open
And it begins teeming

I sit on the porch and watch the rain
I watch the raindrops paint
The walkway to the front door
The rain glazes the asphalt driveway
Until it appears blacker than black

The thunder rolls and the air smells charged
Ozone in the atmosphere around me
Replacing the fragrance of the flowers
Bouncing, dancing, the raindrops strike and merge,
Individual no longer

They are a puddle in the street,
A rivulet racing down the walk,
A reservoir collecting in a leaf,
A tear cascading down a window pane,
Collecting others in its path

Washing, cleansing, making the air preternaturally clear
Everything appears sharp, crisp, clean,

In intense, heightened focus, crystal clarity.
I hear the frogs in the pond across the way
Joining joyously in a wordless chorus

And birds rejoicing in nature's ablution,
Melodious solos, warbled arias here and there
The wind has died and the air is still below
While above, wisps, puffs in blends of gray, blue, white, yellow
Wander languidly across the sky

I love the white noise serenade,
An uninterrupted monotonically mellifluous concerto
As birds and frogs intone counterpoint to the rain,
And I sit quietly mesmerized
As nature's euphonious recital envelopes me

Later, after the rain has subsided and night has descended,
I walk out into my garden
Up and down, end to end, on the damp paver pathway.
I listen to the night's stillness
And drink in the humid serenity

But after a soaking rain, the night is not silent
After a soaking rain, the plants speak,
Whispering of their euphoria
"Behold us. Are we not magnificent? Are we not glorious?
The rain has suffused us, we are enraptured

The sky gives us sun and rain, and we give you pleasure.
And in this, our purpose is fulfilled

Our reason for being is realized."
And as I listen to their moist murmurings,
I thank them, for their beauty, their simplicity, their amity

I praise the plants for their unselfish bequest of delicate elegance
I am beholden to the flowers for their ephemeral gift of beauty
In night's embrace, I am grateful for my garden

———————————————

Retired Lady Leatherneck (US Marine), Renaissance woman, and
a lover of life's mysteries. I'm interested in how others view the
universe, and welcome opportunities to see it through their eyes.
Allpoetry.com/Captain_B2

[Steven McDaniel]

Struggling Author

Caught upon a decision cast between the division of the glistening
argent golden light of the eternal dawn and the relentless primeval
devouring of the eternal void.

Choice between one's own soul is caught within one's own hands
and the hands of those around them.

A soul cannot find peace of mind when their hands around them
see them nothing more than a toy.

Their life will be cast out upon a whim.

Humanity is a word people can find.

Most spend it as if it were a dime.

Time had hopes that our world could change.

The more our world changes the more it stays the same.

Only by our hands can we give hope to those that could not find
it.

For too long has my decision been to sit.

To make a decision to change my life.

At my core I choose to bare this strife.

Uncertainty upon the wind.

My call to be a writer will begin.

_____

I have always enjoyed writing and look forward to working on my
hobby. I enjoy swimming and walking. I like to lift weights as
well. Allpoetry.com/Salem_Macanbhai9

[Peter Morris]

Souls Perfection

As I glance into your eyes and you glance into mine, our souls
start to feel ice cold as if they were dying.
The feeling of death isn't what it appears to be, the truthful
feeling is that of two souls coming together to be complete.

As our souls glance at each other through our eyes reflection, they
now start to feel the true emotions not of death but perfection.

We will never again need to open our eyes to see or feel one
another, as our souls have taken over that position to give us a
clear and persistent vision of our inner perfection.

Our eyes are the mirrors to give our souls their reflection. As we
touch we become the artist that took a blank canvas and painted
our vision of our soul's undeniable perfection.

Born Peter Alexander Morris I live in Richmond Virginia. I love
writing poetry to help those who may have experienced similar
lives. Allpoetry.com/Lyph29

[Judith L Harmon]

Dreams

As I stare out my window I wonder if you are looking out yours at the same time, wishing on the same stars that the distance between us was not far away.

The heartbeats growing ever so faint to everyone else's ears I can still hear as if you were beside me at the frozen moments in time.

I can picture you walking by the clear sands taking in all the familiar sights and sounds of where you call home, Lord I wish I was there with you......

To be there sharing every wondrous thrill, the sun, the sands.... The cool breezes blowing.

I close my eyes as if for one second to be with you if only in my fleeing thoughts.... I can see the sun caressing your body with its warmth, the breezes blowing your hair to and fro, your eyes light up as if for the first time you are seeing this......

And maybe in a way that is just it...seeing things through another's eyes, feeling the thrill of new experiences through another. My eyes tear up just a little, but not for the reasons most would think.

For one moment you and I are one, together sharing our thoughts, feelings, goals..... Then in an instant the glorious feelings start to fade away....

One moment all felt right with the world, no fears...regrets.... Just living life as it was meant to be lived.

I am brought back to the reality that we are yet so far away, half a world away..... Separated by time and distance....

My thoughts that was so clear just mere moments ago are now clouding up as if a gentle storm was coming nearby on its way out to sea.

And the reality that we live is crashing up around me..... I pray that night soon will take me in its embrace called sleep so I May yet again walk by your side if only within... A dream.

_____

Judith was Born in Seattle in 1965, Married & divorced now enjoying being a New grandma to Jack Zeus (2020) (Mother to Shianne, Jack's mom) Son Dakota and two angels. (Shawnee 1996 & Brandon 2012) Allpoetry.com/Judith_Harmon

[Sohini Dutta]

A promise to keep

But I will be with him...
He may not like,
He may not want,
But I will be with him.
He may scream and pout
Express his views aloud,
But I will be with him.

He may want to be left alone
Throw tantrums way beyond
He may fight and yell,
And make the moment intolerable,
But I will be with him.

Life may seem such a burden at first
It will turn into bliss afterwards,
Destiny will flow you in a direction,
Where you least expect to be.
Life will make you beg for peace at times,
But, hang on! You'll be just fine.
Being a mother is like feeling the magic of life
Seeing a part of me, on my outside.
Seeing him grow and learn,
And watching the moments suddenly,
Is so much fun.

I will be by him, watching him always,
Taking care whenever he needs me.
He might complain, on me he might put all blames,
But I will be with him.

My child, until he grows
And even after wisdom sets in,
Till the last moment I breathe,
I just have a promise to keep,
That I will be with him.
Forever, I will be with him.

———————————

I am Sohini Dutta. Originally from India and currently living in
the USA. Poetry for me is a way to express the deepest thoughts in
a mind overwhelmed with emotions. It adds rhythm to life.
Allpoetry.com/Sohini_Dutta

[Christopher L. Leistner]

My One Night Stand

From the bar to her house we scampered along
Thrilled we'd each found a mate,
I gave her a 10, of course we'd been drinking
But still she gave me the 8.

Excited and thinking of what was to come
Not sure of how I'd begin.
We got to the door then she fell to the floor
Before we could even get in.

She fumbled around while still on the ground
Looking for the front door key.
I went down to help my only mistake
Was I got down on just one knee.

She jumped to her feet hands to her mouth
Then screamed out yes yes yes.
And all I could think was no no no
Now how would I get out of this mess.

Still tipsy from wine and a few shots of rum
I said screw it, will you marry me?
She looked at me funny for a second or 2
Saying I thought you had found the door key.

She started to laugh I wanted to cry
I apologized when she said WOW!
But on our 10th year of marriage and 4 kids later
I said who's the one laughing now.

———————————————

AKA Krizly Bear, I was born in Cincinnati, Oh. & grew up in Tx. & Ut. After retiring in Ok. I took up poetry and song writing to fill the void. I enjoy fishing and camping as well as naps outside. Allpoetry.com/Krizly_Bear

[Alwyn Barddylbach]

The Governor

He only listens to what he wants to listen to
and that will never change.
Women will never change him, man nor dog.
Therapy will never change him.
Reason will never change him nor common sense.
Empathy and compassion can't change him
because there is no space for these to grow.
There is no vaccine to protect us from the likes of him;

after the party.

God will never change him,
no justice or angel of peace.
Jen won't change him, no tongues, no prophecy,
no blinding light on the way to Canberra.
He is the epitome of stone,
the lava which spits in your face
as you hand him the keys to heaven.
He attacks anything that moves
in a direction not of his choosing;

after the party,
long live the party dead.

He is a failed managing director
in two countries, the tourism wars.

A liar and public, corporate thief.
He was absent in the thick of the fire,
absent from the crowd that gathered at our door;
ecclesiastical bigot,
the land will never change him,
no wiser or elder evermore;

after the party.

He is a Liberal, the member for Cook,
they gave to us a shadow of the past
and he who stares at us from the dead
he places on the hill.
Misogyny and crocodile tears,
bullets, slogans, sermons, smears.
No cross, stars or serpent sky
will light the path and touch him still;

after the party,
long live the party dead.

Listen to the wisdom of women?
He doesn't even hear himself
and this my friends is our prime minister,
our beloved leader and preacher,
preserver of the colonies,
the one who a handful of bogan
wayward parliamentarian voted for
to maul and govern this country;

after the party,
long live the party,
kiss and cuddle now you're dead.

An ecclesiastical chant and pun, a scandal and scoundrel in every
verse, culture of 'The Party' - Kev said, 'Heads are way dirtier than
teeth', colour the satire! AB, Australia
Allpoetry.com/Barddylbach

[Anna Adams Tauvaa]

Let Go

When I first started understanding life
I tried to kill myself
cutting my wrist with a knife
I hated who I was and who I'd become
each and every day I felt so dumb
Trying my hardest to make my body numb.

_____

I would write because it helped me get all my feelings down
instead of holding it in, it helped me cope with all my inner
feelings that I couldn't really explain or even understand myself,
Allpoetry.com/Msadamsanna

[Lisa F. Raines]

Oh, Descartes!

You are so much more than a brain in a bottle.
I think, therefore I am. What are you if you don't think? What is
thinking?

Is this metaphysical absolutism?
How do we know animals exist?
It's not like the jar brain can gather real experiences.

The Cartesian coordinates system is invaluable,
but is it real? What is real?
Seems like an existential crisis to me.

Can three dimensions can describe all?
A metaphysical construct of the physical,
how does that make the physical real?

Describing the physical only ignores
the metaphysical constructs of love and faith.
Is the immeasurable non-existent?

I think, therefore I am, but what are you?

A mind full of assumed knowledge?
How do you learn if God already
placed everything in your head?

It's arguable that brain needs body to exist
in the physical, 3-D realm you describe
so well with your mathematics.

How do we know your coordinates and
constructs are real? Your existential description
of the metaphysical needs some work.

I think, therefore I question.

Alis Ramie is from North Carolina, USA.
Interests include: philosophy, history, international relations,
poetry, art, design, jazz, funk rock, and some good old soul.
Allpoetry.com/AlisRamie

[Lisa F. Raines]

Was Einstein Wrong?

Regarding E=mc^2
c^2=E/m

Einstein, it's seems to me,
defined, rather arrogantly,
a constant, c,
as the speed of light, and
the fastest any particle can be.

A constant, even squared,
applied across the entirety
of our universe,
seems a bit
presumptuous to me.

To make this distinction,
the heralded equation
must prove true eternally,

anchoring our knowledge
to this simple exchange
of mass and energy.

It seems to be a brilliant theory,
although it is quite deceptive,
as presented in our reality.

In fact, this speed of light,
this limitation, this finite equation,
is only true in a perfect
vacuum situation.

This momentous measurement
changes as light travels
through a medium such as water
or crystal or glass, you see.

Within the same matter,
some highly charged electrons,
CAN move more quickly
than the sacred speed of light.

This difference between the
two speeds can be seen
in the blue light emitted
from Čerenkov radioactivity.

What does that hallowed
equation, the source of
such infatuation, mean,
in a universe full of dark energy?

———————————

Alis Ramie is from North Carolina, USA.
Interests include: philosophy, history, international relations,
poetry, art, design, jazz, funk rock, and some good old soul.
Allpoetry.com/AlisRamie

[Lily Blu]

Deeper than Deep

Are you really you when you look into the mirror? I promise that you are not.

You are a hair out of place or a fuzz on your shoulder. Flaws driven by what others see.

But I ask you, what do you see?

Take a moment to stare deep into your reflection. Gaze past your face, travel beyond your irises and find your soul.

When you look into the mirror what do you see? Is it you or Is it me?

———————————

I've traveled from East to West. I settled for the peace of the sunsets and desert. I write to reflect and remember in beauty. Allpoetry.com/Dreams_of_Rubble

[David I Mayerhoff]

When Man Is the Island

I am an island
in the endless ocean
trying to maintain my identity
without being consumed by the sea

it would be easy to give in
and join the masses
rather than stay in this relentless fight
against gravity, nature and common sense
by asserting my true self

And yet here I am
a sole solitary tree
whose branches have been denuded of all leaves,
whose spirit has been engulfed
by the inevitability of the surrounding conformity

I see in the distance
those who came before me
and those who were my contemporaries
now swimming in the great sea
indistinguishable from that which floats around them

the waves crest against
the small protrusion of land by my feet

as if mocking how hopeless my stance is
and how useless my vision has become

I gain courage and resolve
from these attacks
for I know that deep down
what gives me strength and purpose
is the very fight
that brings the water to my shores
thereby nourishing my roots
to grow into the air and reach the sky
connecting me to the infinite

David I Mayerhoff is an emerging literary writer, established
scientific author, and a Clinical Professor of Psychiatry. He grew
up on Long Island and now resides in New Jersey.
Allpoetry.com/David_Mayerhoff

[Karlie Capozzoli]

mayday! mayday!

violet shadows hover
over pure white bed sheets
and upon the vanity,
candles flutter in the setting sun.

i gently shift the drapes
and the last drop of sunlight
glows onto the stained wood
of the perched ottoman.

carefully carved window sills
and extravagant linens
are settled beneath me,
as delicate as a darling rose.

oh captain of my soul,
i pour just one more glass
to forget, to hide, to feel
something? or nothing?

i take teeny tiny sips
just to scorch my throat,
the same way you ignite fire
within my pitied soul.

your flame engulfs me
like a turbulent sinking ship,
self destructing into a void
of nothingness.

mayday! mayday!
my broken heart yearns for more
as i drown within
the harsh reality of us.

i stare at my glinting glass
and wait endlessly
for the tides to push me
closer to you.

oh captain of my soul,
i take another pull
and overthink (sink, sink, sink)
some more.

i drink, drink, drink
as i wonder, worry, ware
myself fucking out
with mindless matters.

oh captain of my soul!
throw me overboard!
i beg you to put me
at fucking ease.

oh captain of my soul,
i desire calmer seas...
i desire
you and me.

Karlie is originally from Baltimore, but resides in Minneapolis,
MN. She writes poetry and performs with hula hoops to express
herself creatively. Karlie loves the Transcendentalists and
Modernists. Allpoetry.com/Karliekat

Printed in Great Britain
by Amazon